COMMUNIST SPIRIT

They're Mean Meddlers Too

Karen Kellock Ph.D.

Manual for Superior Men

A complete theory based on Einstein physics, Political Psychology, Systems Theory and Archetypal Psychiatry.

FORMULA

All success attraction
All disease obstruction
All recovery elimination

You must fast on all three

OBSTRUCTIONS:

People
Habit
Food

COMMUNIST SPIRIT

Leech defined: Sticky fingers, sucking spirit. Communist spirit: if you have three and I have one you *owe* me one: liberals are terrible/no fun. When encountering the communist spirit run the other way or quickly put up your boundaries. Covetousness is common so stop giving away your possessions. People respect you/your things. The ability to say NO without feeling selfish is about boundaries so start practicing this.

forward to COMMUNIST SPIRIT

ADAPTATION BECOMES NEUROTIC STYLE

In childhood there's an unpredictable adult who is risky and the sensitive empath takes in everything.

One must be hyper-attuned to the risky adult and after a life of this you're insane not just a nut.

The empath became hyper-attuned to anything in the room that's no-ok and that's his style today.

How one adapts becomes his neurotic style: now everything makes sense like why he's hostile.

The empath is filled with shame but that's only cuz the others poured all their bad into him ok.

She tries hyper-perfect to not cause them to hurt her again--that means hyper-attuned to him.

It's enmeshment flash: being totally aware of everything in the room, a slave to trash.

ENMESHMENT

Enmeshment: no boundaries, we pick up/take on other's feelings into our own personality.

Walking on eggshells: if they're upset, she's upset and anything about her own reality she'll forget.

Narcissists: there's a moment when fear leaves their eyes and anger becomes their driver, aye.

The turbulence and unpredictability brought survival stress that tore down your body baby.

You must rest now: essential R & R after this war and fight for survival as your heart was torn.

forward to COMMUNIST SPIRIT

Narcissistic people see constant forgiveness as acceptance so they create more mess.

They like to test the waters and push your boundaries to see what they can be forgiven for see.

Once learning the key symptoms, no narc stands a chance against an empowered empath.

The narc won't accept boundaries cuz it takes away their control. They'll agree then get bold.

Setting boundaries is the easy part, enforcing them is impossible as their insecurities start up.

RUTHLESSNESS

Note a narc's ruthless behavior in discard stage. That alone bashes self-worth even in old age.

His wonderful gestures at the beginning have disappeared forever, that's the bummer.

You begin to feel conscious and uncomfortable in your own skin from criticisms according to him.

They think everyone is a cheater and liar like them. He says "who are you dressing up for" again.

You have ulterior motives or trying to attract attention: that's his view from pure projection.

An example of parasitic takeover: coaching her on how to present herself but jealous if she's clever.

Giving or withholding approval is for the hijacking of a personality by a narcissistic person see.

She gives up--on makeup or anything else. Now he criticizes her for being unkept or ugliness.

forward to COMMUNIST SPIRIT

Your body in a narc relationship keeps massive score of the trauma of being betrayed and gaslit.

You're getting sick from the constant confusion 24/7 and the survival mode you're forced to be in.

The narc says and feels whatever's in his head at the moment but then he promptly forgets it.

Savior complex of narcs: you think how could he be so evil when he's so helpful to strangers?

INSTENSITY WITHOUT LONGEVITY

There's intensity to whatever pops into his head but there's no longevity: he forgets it all instead.

When he gets bored, in contradiction or feels attacked he acts on impulse and drops his mask.

"Harmless jokes" slowly undermine your confidence. They aren't funny, it's just another nuisance.

He puts you and your work down thru plausible deniability. You then recall your faults see.

They are poison wrapped in honey: it tastes sweet but feels bitter--mixed signals indicate treachery.

Something's harming you but you can't figure out what: that's life with a covert narcissist: no luck.

The narc leaves you in a mixed emotional state and this confused darkness ruins your entire day.

Don't push it, take a vacation. Never force the fit just relax and with holy spirit ease it gets done.

Nothing done, yet nothing left undone. It just all gets finished when you're living right with God.

forward to COMMUNIST SPIRIT

Decision: spend time with people who are violent and nasty in nature or with the kind and mature?

Some are loving and giving by their nature. People present to us what they are so stay aware.

You're never on equal playing field with a narcissist and their goal is to stay one-up so forget it sis.

When you're feeling good about yourself they gotta bring you down and anyway they can man.

The more you put into a toxic relationship the less you get out of it and those are the dynamics.

NO RETURN ON INVESTMENT

Ask: What is the return on this investment? Are you getting anything from this relationship?

Gossip-called-concern marks a sick system. Women are slandering their husbands esp. in Al Anon.

When you're focused on the narcissist you miss other opportunities and lose yourself too sis.

You lose self-love and IDENTITY--what you have goin' on--because of your obsession with a man.

Don't dismay when they spread their wings for before you know it they'll be mowed down see.

It goes right to their head and they make BIG mistakes--like virtue signaling rather than truth ok.

EXTRAS

Vitamin K2 prevents calcium buildup in arteries. It's found in animal protein/FAT: meat and cheese.

forward to COMMUNIST SPIRIT

Federal law prohibits entry of communists into the U.S. yet they're coming in cuz we're borderless.

They always say they're coming for the rich but soon it's you because it's always a bait and switch.

Bidenomics: shaking down other countries for bribes and getting the media to cover for ya, aye.

The best ideas win when no ideas are censored. Otherwise it's tyranny over minds for sure.

Don't push it. Creativity happens naturally & when it hits you're compelled to joyously finish it.

SOCIAL HYPNOSIS

UP AND AWAY: PTSD BALLOON IMAGE
DON'T GO INTO SPAM
WOMEN WHO CHASE MEN
WOMEN ARE PRIZE NOT PREY
HE LOVES YOU AS A FUNCTION
LOVE YOUR PETS DESPITE DANDER
TRAUMA AND MORAL/BOUNDARY COLLAPSE
SHUN PROFANE AND IDLE BABBLE
WOLVES IN SHEEPS CLOTHING
THE PRIZE DOESN'T SHOOT HER SHOT
THE OLD YOUNG AND YOUNG OLD
FEMALE COLLUSIONS
OLDER WOMEN/YOUNGER MEN
WERE BOOMER MEN MEAN TO WOMEN?
NO GIFTS AND YOU DON'T PAY
DON'T GET IN THEIR CAR
MASS TDS SYNDROME IN WIVES
THE INSANE ALCOHOLIC ENVIRONMENT
AGE GAP RELATIONSHIPS
DON'T LET EM INTO YOUR HOUSE
NEXT TYRANNY PHASE
PHYSICAL MALADIES
REVERSAL DIETING IS THE SOLUTION
CAN YOU SWITCH INTO DETOX?
COMPLETION OF THE CREATIVE ACT

SOCIAL HYPNOSIS

A discoverer brings Creative Act to the earth. It seeds, germinates and completes [gives birth].

To teachers and sages: When due respect becomes dense disruption, drop em and start again.

You haven't been truthful enough. Pulling back to not offend when you shoulda been rough.

What made us crazy? Other people. We woulda been fine alone, creative children happy and normal..

People are so cruel I can still hear them yelling at me. They imprinted early/I survived treachery.

UP AND AWAY: PTSD BALLOON IMAGE

You have PTSD memories of being invaded ok. Envision a big air balloon taking you UP and AWAY.

You keep churning/chewing the same conversations of 30 years ago. Balloon: up and away, NO GO.

It's fruitless: You had no assertion powers then so it frustrates the hell out of you now, looking back.

These thought loops do not serve you and wreck entire days. Conserve your time: BALLOON ok.

How can you settle it or get "closure" if they're dead, in a rest home or don't even remember?

They think you're hot stuff but it's only cuz you want privacy and appear aloof/WAY above.

Actually you're bored to death with these people who are using you and I went thru this too.

SOCIAL HYPNOSIS

Up, up and away--you'll never see em again: pray God takes everything from your spirit, amen.

You had no business nor desire to be with these people to begin with--you were PUSHED into it.

You were MISADVISED by your "friends" and down the rabbit hole you went, wasting time again.

After envisioning the magic balloon, hear a freeway with you speeding way ahead to the future soon.

Your PTSD memories are of what it's like dealing with the herd. You're an elite now/no profit here.

Don't get mad just file it away. You'll be given a chance to make it right or give em hell to pay.

Incredible ambition comes from either being rejected as a child or loved and encouraged as valuable.

Sly innuendos and half truths. that's the way the social leader puts you down, the one who's new.

Early traumas were part mental illness, part drunkeness and the fact I couldn't stand liberals.

Having introjected a brawling alcoholic I became her yelling like a lunatic. I recognize this.

DON'T GO INTO SPAM

To build strength, don't check your spam folder. Recall they're scum/thought they were better.

To test your resolve, don't check spam. Remember these were scum questioning you ma'am.

Here's the truth: you gotta forgive em to get em outa your system. Otherwise you rot, not them.

SOCIAL HYPNOSIS

They're in your spam folder for a reason so don't go fishin', its easy to slip back while cruisin'.

Close old doors so new ones can open and STAY open. Don't go fishin'/relapsin' for any reason.

You should be afraid to go into spam. It's a dark cavern aiming to hurt/reject/discount you man.

In that one event I found out I was a speaker and with massive effects. Adolf Hitler

WOMEN WHO CHASE MEN

Women are reduced to chasing after self-esteem's been shattered by society thru relationship.

Women are the prize, not supposed to be out there shootin' their shot trying to win some guy.

The lie: man will take the pain away/make you whole, and a broken sisterhood confirms it all.

Advised by broken friends she's coached to be desperate and he lets her chase cuz he's a wreck.

A man broken in his masculinity lacks capacity to supply her deficiency, he makes it worse see.

He sees her as prey so it's a rabbit chasing a lion then spat out afterwards: get real hon'.

The chaser [pursuer] is immediately put into emotional vulnerability by the pursued.

The pursuer must WAIT for the pursued to approve or not. That's not being a queen you nut.

If a woman' chases a man she's holding her breath cuz if he rejects what happens to her heart, eh?

SOCIAL HYPNOSIS

It is a healthy queen's honor to approve or disapprove. Not to be trashed and treated like a fool.

It's never God's intention for his daughter to run a man down: "it's disgusting" Melania frowns.

The worst happens if chaser catches the chased. He'll either spit out the prey or give her hell to pay.

It's unnatural for a man to reject a woman because she put herself in that position--it's disgustin'.

This is why rejection hits so hard in a woman, she was never meant to be in that position.

A man who can approve, or disapprove? That's why it takes many years off a woman's heart too.

WOMEN ARE PRIZE NOT PREY

By the Creator women were designed as the prize. A man finds a good thing and favor, aye.

Women are the prize, not supposed to be out there shootin' their shot trying to win the prize.

Chasing allows/manages the female to be used as a tool. That's why men are often for it too.

Chasing is a false concept in the hands of a perverted generation of men saying they love it.

God never designed you for a position to be emotionally vulnerable. Chasing men is awful.

It's God: He puts a bee in your bonnet and you go with it then get your husband on it: perfect.

The most profitable time is music and thought. And of course pet therapy, i.e. cats and dogs.

SOCIAL HYPNOSIS

We're being replaced as we speak. A flood like you've never seen all planned by Joe Biden see.

Let your image come to mind, never force it on them. You're through with chasing even friends.

Music/dreaming comes first **THEN** your other learning devices. It's the inner realm you guys.

A queen is chosen not doing the chasing so in the meantime just do your thing, not in waiting.

Doesn't it feel good to be free of him? To not view everything thru his lens? Heaven.

HE LOVES YOU AS A FUNCTION

He loves you for the function you fulfill, it's not about you. A narcissist can't see beyond self Sue.

He's real excited at first but gets bored easily and distracts to something/someone else.

Wishing and hoping he'll choose me, since I'm just an option not number one, the only one.

"If she says **ONE** more thing I disagree with I'm gonna drop her and ruin her reputation quick."

With every chemical injury you become more sensitive and isolated in your own bubble see.

Wishing and hoping he'll choose you, are you kidding? You do the choosing honey.

Don't remember water under the bridge, only how it ends up. Smelling like a rose/on top.

Eat as much as you want on the break-fast plan and each day it'll be less as things settle up.

SOCIAL HYPNOSIS

They come in to use you for info then end up calling you a racist or putting you down somehow.

Stop inciting cat abuse man. There's an anti-female slant: if they can't kill her they'll kill her cat.

LOVE YOUR PETS DESPITE DANDER

For the chemically sensitive, pet dander is like being in a gas chamber: you must have purifiers.

Air purifiers remove 99% of pet dander: don't eliminate your pets just get clear/get this gear.

I love my pets but I couldn't breathe. Dam dander clogs up the atmosphere and I was sick see.

I blamed everything else but dander. It's a blind spot when it comes to pets/get a purifier.

The blinds are filled with dander. I need detail cleaning now and then be clear and healthy later.

Love your cats and dogs, it's not their fault. They'll be healthier too when the purifier is on.

I got off the I Can Eat Anything trip in order to save my pets: lower total load= no dander effects.

Break free from food routines and habits. You can fly now, sometimes it'll be days you forgot it.

TRAUMA AND MORAL/BOUNDARY COLLAPSE

With trauma there is moral and boundary collapse. There's no defense and you can't fight back.

The victim cannot assert or defend himself. Accusations take hold though they are false.

SOCIAL HYPNOSIS

The traumatized victim could be silenced for decades, unable to explain himself: he's muted ok.

There's nothing more damaging than entertaining false friends: sabotaging peace of mind/becoming less.

Acquaintances, partners, neighbors, other members: none of that is friendship, it's far stronger.

Many will party with you but few will go to battle with you: the test of truth and longevity too.

A friend has our best interest/sticks around when times get tough. They aren't made but discovered.

Friendship is a natural resource that cannot be fabricated. It either happens or is truncated.

SHUN PROFANE AND IDLE BABBLE

Shun profane and idle babble, which increases to ungodliness and spreads like cancer. Tim 2:16

You tease apart fine differences, they misjudge everything you say as offensive/I'm sick of this.

You complain about society, they call you ungrateful cuza all you have, they don't get it see.

Pets are a slice of innocence/unconditional love in this cold cruel world so our dreams unfurl.

I knew she was a ruby as she's the only one who didn't throw herself at me. Happy husband

The biggest obstruction to female genius is the female community itself. They hate novelty/envious.

She's touchy and prickly and a definite obstruction to you honey, better to be alone all day.

SOCIAL HYPNOSIS

So unself-aware she can't accept her foibles so blames him for being noncommittal that's all.

I suffered being a baby boomer. I hated swimming in muddy waters with hippies and whatever.

Feigning sickness as a compensatory gesture so they won't feel threatened, like a system restore.

Jesus said: many will come in my name--MANY. It's a wide path to hell and a narrow one to heaven see.

WOLVES IN SHEEPS CLOTHING

Some call themselves Christians but they are wolves in sheep's clothing so don't listen to em.

I didn't like women after that. I saw em all as dominating tyrannical inferior thinkers/fact.

If she doesn't like you/what you say she'll ruin your rep today and look so sweetly innocent ok.

The emotional cut off from old/sick systems eliminates all symptoms. That's the link then.

When someone's in your home you gotta adapt to their personality/agenda: don't let em in momma!

The lowlife is sickened by his lowness so compensates by bringing down your highness.

Regarding past: you had to build a legend somehow--of course it was low to contrast to you now.

I hated how he always beckoned to women--the alpha females running the show in total control.

Those alpha females hate creative women. They wanna control everything you do or say vermin.

SOCIAL HYPNOSIS

They're out to get a man so chase/lock him up thru sex but how will you keep him now sis?

How will you keep his attention [let alone win his love] with you acting like an aging slut?

THE PRIZE DOESN'T SHOOT HER SHOT

The PRIZE doesn't shoot her shot for some guy! Be wife material, chaste, then YOU choose, aye.

Some act according to the godly impulse inside, some act according to the traditions of men, aye.

They already pegged him as bad so no matter what she said without judge nor jury, ht's dead.

Don't know why God chose this vessel for the Creative Act, an actual structure in nature in fact.

All I can smell is sawdust or dander depending on the weather. My sensitivities change/bummer.

Each time we're zapped [chemically injured] the range of stimuli making us sick increases/gets worse.

Your sensitivities get wider, the families of chemicals bigger until you're in a teardrop trailer.

Email: Answer when convenient, you have a record and most importantly you aren't interrupted.

THE OLD YOUNG AND YOUNG OLD

So much went on in his young life that he was very deep early on and could relate like an adult.

The great relationship ends cuz they don't communicate or wanna walk thru all that: what a shame.

SOCIAL HYPNOSIS

All the stuff you went thru was for resilience, strength and even style. The velvet glove/you got it now.

Unrealized ones are enmeshed in the system, blind to it, a mindless cog in the undifferentiated blob.

When we self-realize all hell breaks loose--in the form of sly innuendos, stupid cruelty and half truths.

"I was so hurt around em, thinking who are these people, I can't stand them!" Cured patient

They love you one day then talk to their group who hate then trash you the next day: unstable mates.

FEMALE COLLUSIONS

Having talked with her friends she's turned against you and it's obvious: don't fight this, start again.

When she arrived it was obvious she'd talked with her friends again. An irritable witch/put downs.

Though he was a drunken wino he was a brilliant social manipulator so everyone blamed HER.

Before my Ph.D. in the Streets I had no idea what people were like but I'm a recluse now, aye.

Ask any Holocaust survivor what people are like. That people are good and nice is a big dam lie.

The wife of the alcoholic usually ends up in the blamed position. I was there, it was SO frustratin'.

Stop calling people "good". Jesus said "Don't call me good, only God is good." Understood?

Even wives of alcoholics took the wino's side. God forbid they side with the poor blamed wife.

SOCIAL HYPNOSIS

They knew what she went through and STILL sided with the husband: cogs in the wheel/sexism.

OLDER WOMEN/YOUNGER MEN

The world is changing people, we must expand our concepts: the older woman has been ditched.

I felt so abused by a baby boomer cad I said to Heavenly Dad: I'll take ANYTHING else but that.

After she's a certain age, discard her--and anyone with her has an agenda: as perceived by culture.

Why they hate age gap relationships with the women older? We're valued for youth and beauty sir.

Living in broken consciousness made me weak, weaselly and sick: be bold, do your thing quick.

The older guys are mean to women, discounting and ugly too. The young guys pop up: "I want you!"

The older guys are mean to women, discounting and ugly too but the young guys say: "I want you!"

The guys your age pass you up for age as if you're inferior while the young men only admire.

WERE BOOMER MEN MEAN TO WOMEN?

The boomer men put you down as if aging is a disease but the young ones say: you're my queen!

I couldn't believe how the old man treated me: as if he owned me, without empathy, psychopathy.

Maybe young men saw what they didn't like in their fathers, and evolved to maturity quicker.

SOCIAL HYPNOSIS

"A younger man relationship was my healing after a traumatic relationship giving me PTSD."

Who wants to be trashed/cast aside for age? If younger men love you for it change your mate.

They go to strip clubs and pay for attention then actually believe it. They can do this.

If I had to pay for attention I'd feel rotten but men are able to justify even while hitting bottom.

Something you can't help--being over 30--and they put you down for it? Go no contact and love it.

NO GIFTS AND YOU DON'T PAY

An older woman who pays for the young man is enabling him to not be successful: none of that girl.

You'd be teaching him that climbing up is always over someone else, ever at the whim of others.

I don't like gigolos and see any man coming to a woman for money as weak, pathetic and low.

Having been raised by female bosses that work, young men love and adore an alpha female sir.

DON'T GET IN THEIR CAR

Murdered/tortured females got in Ted Bundy's car. He was handsome, well spoken, nice dressin'.

Enantiodromia: everything converts to it's opposite--least likely to succeed becomes president.

WHY do they side with the alcoholic husband? Because of how the wife's actin'--sicker than him.

SOCIAL HYPNOSIS

The wife's mal-adaptation to alcoholism makes her sicker than her husband: scapegoatism.

Her disparagement of God and patriots made me sick. Angry liberal/who does she think she is?

MASS TDS SYNDROME IN WIVES

Wife called Trump "despicable". What does she think she is? Her poor husband, a Trump disciple.

The wives are ugly with TDS and it brings his disgust but he's too nice to confront so just adjusts.

How could the wives hate one who put America on it's zenith and love the destroyers following it?

When Janis Joplin went back home they only came against her and she felt doubly alone.

Why do I hear people yelling at me? That's the plight of a nonconformist: past voices inside see.

I can still see their angry faces, how I feared their violence and how false their accusations.

The solution is to create your own bubble, stay away from the rabble and with friends be careful.

THE INSANE ALCOHOLIC ENVIRONMENT

Living in an alcoholic environment is so diminishing to the person I caved in, not knowing.

The added insult of people coming against me--as if I was the problem--drove me down, amen?

They love you at first then collude with their friends and come back like a different person.

SOCIAL HYPNOSIS

When this happens it's as if their friends are in the room. No triangulations, just be alone.

Not all men get better with age by transforming to self-aware mature men: age doesn't - wisdom.

AGE GAP RELATIONSHIPS

In an age gap relationship you must both be aligned against the outer world criticizing it.

It's about a vibration. There are very young old people and very old young people: ageism is evil.

We cave in thru lowered self-worth: it stays in your craw, wrecks your sleep, creeps into thoughts.

At the end I can say I ran the race and completed my task ok--but will it meet with high pay?

Vacillation, degradation, false accusation, minimization, and other rude devices by them: reject em.

Comparisons and putting you in competition: we've discussed the aging effects of gamin'.

So don't give men money or gifts and have enough self-worth to just sit. It's your home/you're legit.

People yelling at me: perhaps God's training in some way. To be ready/armored/not so trusting.

DON'T LET EM INTO YOUR HOUSE

Don't let them into your house for the sake of the PETS. That is their environment too you twit.

The narcissistic mother makes daughter afraid to set boundaries from her urgent need to please.

NEXT TYRANNY PHASE

SOCIAL HYPNOSIS

Next tyranny phase: arrest warrants for opposition leaders including comedians and journalists.

Historic year: record crime, inflation, illegal border crossings, gas prices and market losses.

We're being turned into mutants. The vaccines mutate the genes and are passed to all generations.

PHYSICAL MALADIES

Millions die each year of choking in their sleep, asphyxiating. That's cuz they ate dinner see.

Just skip dinner to save your life. When sleeping it comes up and asphyxiates in the throat, aye.

Dander or sawdust is all I smell all day depending on the weather which changes sensitivities.

Two big purifiers in the room and I'm still sick. God help us what are they spraying, the lunatics?

The lower desert was dry, this is much greener and it means pollen/dander alerts and spores.

Body shoots out acid, acting as a buffer like an air bag against these CHEMICALS so murderous.

We're living in a gas chamber and for the sensitive it's asphyxiating and also painful: deadly killers.

No more mono-mania or orthorexia. I eat what I want but I know how to fix it/return to utopia.

Couple sticks of shortbread and I'm done for the day. Anything more and it's hell to pay.

Selfix Smoothie [sip for two days]: 7 bananas, bag frozen mango chunks, bag super greens ok.

SOCIAL HYPNOSIS

I eat whatever the hell I want but I have selfix/detox reversals lest I stray too far off/bloat up.

REVERSAL DIETING IS THE SOLUTION

Reversal dieting cuz you know the facts: That's where it's at--not mono-mania or rigid diets lass.

If I don't eat I don't burp, have bubbles, suffer acid reflux or choke in my sleep: love to fast.

Controlling diet was the key to lowering total load--so I could live with my pets: budget of gold.

I got off the I Can Eat Anything trip in order to save my pets: lower total load= no dander effects.

If I eat donuts made with soy oil, up goes total load and later there's no escape from the turmoil.

To keep my pets I must control diet then total load goes way down and by dander I won't be hit.

Does meat raise immunity or total load--doing the opposite see? Health is clean/sick is dirty.

CAN YOU SWITCH INTO DETOX?

Can you even switch back to detox for a few days, or too far gone on this addictive craze?

Alcoholism is not just a few beers. It's a disease, genetic and anosognosic: in denial for sure.

Alcoholism is not being able to cease once having started: in a train to hell you're strapped.

The added insult of people coming against me--as if I was the problem--drove me down, amen?

SOCIAL HYPNOSIS

Chemical sensitivity is like living in a gas chamber. It's a hellish life but for survival we live simpler.

COMPLETION OF THE CREATIVE ACT

Teleported to the next dimension by becoming one with the holy spirit. This is done as you repent.

If my genotype is for oration--to speak with effects on the nation--I feel so blessed/it is grace son.

The **BEST** saints **WERE** the worst sinners. Keep that in your thoughts, rid remorse and be winners.

THE COMMUNIST SPIRIT
is a Bagashit

CONSTANT INTERRUPTIONS IN SOCIAL CULTURE
THE SOCIAL IS POWERFUL
AMERICANA AND CHRISTIANITY IS FREEDOM
INVADERS CREEP INTO HOUSES
DEGRADED BY INFERIOR MEN
ALWAYS FOR THE GOOD OF THE WHOLE
HIGH CONFIDENCE FOR WHAT?
LOW VALUE WOMEN
SHE'S MAD SO SHE'S RIGHT
UNRESOLVED TRAUMA
KEEP HIM IN SPAM, IGNORE IT THEN
OLDER WOMEN KNOW BUDDY
SEE HIM AS THE DEVIL
MY ASIAN FEMALE BODY TYPE
LITTLE GIRL OR MAGNETISM?
STOP STUFFING

THE COMMUNIST SPIRIT
is a Bagashit

The degradation from inferior men is infinite so it is hard to forget it once going thru it, but do it.

He didn't even deserve a conversation but the clown in a crown took control by driving her down.

He demanded I do what he wanted all for the good of the whole and I told him to stuff it.

READING: Stop ever-learning but never coming to the truth. Gain wisdom by enjoying the view.

She's a thoroughbred, an aristocrat. Man, you don't play head games with someone like that.

Your insides are far more revealing than any book since it's all about you and God not a potluck.

You will be valued as you value yourself. He will soon hate you for putting up with his stuff.

Stiff upper lip and a square jaw: you've reached the limit of what you can take and allowed.

He doesn't love you, doesn't care and not meant for you so why chase that man who's stupid too?

Leave the foe flattened: that was my intention before I realized it's a spiritual war with Satan.

CONSTANT INTERRUPTIONS IN SOCIAL CULTURE

Your auto-responders to cultural programming will die down. Don't be defensive/have self-love.

THE COMMUNE IS A BAGASHIT

If always responding to interruptions you're not in control of your day. YOU plan/they stay away.

In progressive America no one stands out, that wouldn't be fair. Those who do will get there's.

Everything is cheap and gross, everyone gets an award. No one stands out or they're attacked/ignored.

If always responding to interruptions you're not in control of your day. YOU plan/they stay away.

It's that communist spirit: that the social [good of the whole] is more important than being alone.

You must give up your independence and freedom to do what YOU want, for the "good of the whole."

The communist spirit [commune-mess] is the opposite to Americana and Christianity: the INDIVIDUAL.

They're so social they'll bring a gang to your house without asking, to them it's so normal.

They drill away till they find your soft spot then have a field day with it: they are ill bred rot.

THE SOCIAL IS POWERFUL

People think they can get in and get out and not be affected but you can't isolate/separate it.

Men can compartmentalize but women are integrated and one act effects her whole framework.

It's true the best talents ripen late: those bringing the most people to God and the True Self ok.

We all have our day of public humiliation when we're knocked down a notch for our good son.

THE COMMUNE IS A BAGASHIT

Everything you do and every decision you make should start with "this will affect eternity for me".

But you left the design of tradition and suffered the world of controversy and disdain my son.

To not conform demands you be a battleship to defend your freedom, which is your privacy/home.

Freedom to live the way YOU want to and not conform to the group for it's tyrannical/don't stoop.

AMERICANA AND CHRISTIANITY IS FREEDOM

Just cuz Christianity is about freedom of the individual a church may not be. I felt extremely unfree.

They expected me to attend boring social events which had nothing to do with God--no thanks.

They didn't like a life's work taking up all my time but Christ would support such devotion, aye.

The communist spirit creeped me out since kindergarten. I got homesick for home again.

School phobia set in and I just wanted to stay home. To this day I hate groups and ALL socials.

Social: a waste of time and boring as hell cuz NOTHING approaches the true self, the inner citadel.

Social gives em a chance to take pot shots at you. Don't be a sitting duck, be alone and pursue.

Get ready to be called antisocial, a hater and rude. Who cares, these are losers or they'd be busy too.

Learning clever repartees was my way of handling it before. Ridiculous, be alone and explore.

THE COMMUNE IS A BAGASHIT

Work till you die but retire early: by separating from society's structures of social expectancy.

It's like prison: not safe to be a lone ranger, you gotta group up for protection. Get with God son.

It's like an entire generation felt entitled to your time, money and body but the boomers are leaving.

Don't get in the hole of not being extremely wealthy or you may find yourself a slave honey.

So you can keep your life running no matter what, not depending on people, the biggest block.

That's WHY financial security is so important: it gives you independence from the merciless.

INVADERS CREEP INTO HOUSES

An invader creeping into your house can ruin your life and your family. Caveat one: keep em out.

What's yours is yours and you don't have to share it. That's just an excuse to loot, believe it.

If they don't want your money/body it's your TIME, the most valuable commodity so keep em out, aye.

Years I lost to the locust: creepy invaders of home just wanting to hang cuz I was a good hostess.

When God was done with my wilderness experience he yanked me outa my cabin into a mansion.

He insults her in private so everyone thinks the wife of the alki is the mean one and alcoholic.

We never make a decision against what's good for us to save a relationship with a man: get this!

THE COMMUNE IS A BAGASHIT

DEGRADED BY INFERIOR MEN

Cuza your weak comportment they took over and drove you down. Forget this to now be renowned.

Memories of being degraded by inferior men stays locked in your head. Forget and win instead.

She actually didn't know any better than to entertain inferior men just because they wanted in.

A narcissist is shallow. Because he already knows it all nothing gets in and he's SO boring too doll.

The narcissist never gets beyond self so stays shallow. It's ALL about him:. on and on he goes.

ALWAYS FOR THE GOOD OF THE WHOLE

If it's always for the good of the whole they don't mind killing off a couple million, that's the thinkin'

What do you mean "where's it written"? Look at the facts, open your eyes to the self-evident.

You made a desperate appeal now save your breath. Go back to your cage, with God engage instead.

Let God wash memory. He doesn't want you hurt by negative thoughts even for true history.

The question is not why you got hurt by them, but why you were so unprotected/trusted em?

God, wash the past. Illuminate the best and when it comes to bad block it out/give me a rest.

I died of boredom from his shallowness. It put me in a mental wasteland tho' seeming glamorous.

THE COMMUNE IS A BAGASHIT

Suffocating in shallowness: Tried to get meaning from him but there was no depth/just ignorance.

A low value woman has delusionally big sense of who she is. She doesn't add but thinks she does.

The "independent" ["a man can't handle me"] girl is also delusional but also massively entitled.

Tho' coming from an average family she's extremely spoiled and entitled expecting it all see.

In her mind she's a queen but to the world she's average. She's looking for a king, to change.

HIGH CONFIDENCE FOR WHAT?

High confidence unmatched by true value is an unagreeable turnoff to men of high value.

They're full of visions of possibilities while men look at the probable, a far more grounded reality.

No one wants to deal with unrealistic expectations or entitled desires and boundary invasions.

Low women play games with men they see as beneath them. They are testy, making men chase em.

LOW VALUE WOMEN

They operate in grey areas--you'd be attacked for the same but she's always flirting with others.

She operates in drama and gossip because it makes her feel so POWERFUL to create such chaos.

The low value woman insults and shames others. She treats the waiter poorly/gossips forever.

THE COMMUNE IS A BAGASHIT

They compare their men to high value actors or athletes just to make them feel weak and effete.

In her delusion she feels entitled to the lifestyle of others and disdains her husband forever.

Being weaker a low value woman relies on inflicting emotional pain to control the game.

They'll put down the man because of his height, lost goals or other things out of his control.

A low value woman is loud and inarticulate. Yelling, screaming: her feelings rule and that's it.

SHE'S MAD SO SHE'S RIGHT

She's feels RAGE so she's right and you don't dare to explain otherwise and are in for a bad night.

Low value women lack the ability to communicate effectively and efficiently and are rather silly.

She lacks ability to chain ideas and explain them for solutions--she's an in-your-face woman.

Since she'll do anything he begins to feel like a prisoner, a cat in a roomful of rocking chairs.

He would suffocate in shallowness were it not for the constant vacillations in the environment.

She who does not eat deserves to have everything laid at her feet so I say: fast to be an elite.

They can't stop eating their feelings/lack discipline to self-motivate and get into physical shape.

An out of shape woman is low value being more likely to experience debility and disease and soon.

THE COMMUNE IS A BAGASHIT

It's all under her control to be in the best shape possible: obesity is a red flag to men/most all.

Far more people die of obesity complications than hunger and the rich are active and slender.

Low value women are trashy, not elegant. Society values women with grace and self-respect.

Trashy, pugnacious behavior brings on like results. Women need to wake up and be adults.

UNRESOLVED TRAUMA

Unresolved trauma of the past is glaring in a woman of low caste--a burden til worked thru at last.

Troubled, damaged women are high-maintenance and that's just reality to any man at a glance.

She will require patience, time and effort far beyond a healthy relationship and a wise man knows it.

It's a cost someone will bare just to be with her. Her friends too eventually give up and turn.

Someone without this work to be done will excel in work, find a good loving man and have fun.

We're not responsible for abuse in the past but are for healing and success, from repentance.

Controlling, jealous, unable to show trust. Casts doubt on what is said and spies on phones a lot.

One excels in work without such baggage, attracting a good man and having great advantage.

If you wanna be a female leader, study the men--not what's in your head or what your sister said.

THE COMMUNE IS A BAGASHIT

As far as nutrition goes, do what is best for you. You already know this and it's fasting for a few.

Dem's idea of democracy: 80% of Americans want to close the border but it's wide open see.

I suffocated in his shallowness. Lord in heaven is this all there is I asked? I escaped into abundance.

KEEP HIM IN SPAM, IGNORE IT THEN

If you hate him enough to put him in spam you keep him there and never check it again ma'am.

No-contact means you finally getting self-control. You don't go there again, you don't search him.

Learn to love yourself by finally saying NO to what you despise and yet never thought about.

Let this be a test of your self-love while making gold. This story's getting old, repent and be bold.

If you put someone in spam that means you never go there to "see" or whatever's your plan.

You can sneak around and lurk over this clown but it wastes time/proves you haven't grown.

For every time you refuse to lurk/search you've grown an inch in your character, like a church.

Make gold, build character and dust off your hands. You see the evil man now get away fast.

God rescued you before and He will now. Close the old door and He'll give you a new life: wow!

Be a lady for once. Don't search spam and don't go to where he's at--physical or station.

THE COMMUNE IS A BAGASHIT

Thank you Father for rescuing me again. It's a blessing to call on the Solution: my only Friend.

She says "kill a cow and eat it to lose weight". How un-female spirit can you get, a disgusting trait.

Don't check your spam folder, build character and continue not-doing what you used to.

The clowns don't even deserve a conversation with you. Put em in spam and forget those dudes.

OLDER WOMEN KNOW BUDDY

An elder woman knows MEN at all levels of maturity and won't put up with it even in the elderly.

Stay in his matrix and endure all he has planned for you, getting worse/more painful each time too.

When you truly and finally break up there is no letter. Not one word, it's all been said before.

God said in prayer: the more you avoid the gross pig the more I'll give you something new/fresher.

You knew the guy from the outset but didn't trust your instincts so here you are, in the dumps.

When you finally see the light about a guy don't keep telling it, just drop it/don't give it energy.

It's just like he's sitting in your room. That's his influence & conquest if you think of the dude.

In your relationships with people you can be taken for quite a ride. It can take decades/you can die.

Narcissistic abuse is primarily emotional at the hands of someone with no empathy for you at all.

THE COMMUNE IS A BAGASHIT

You're treated that way by HIM--not everyone--so don't get paranoid on me just walk away now hon'.

Bible says "give no place to the devil" and seeing the narcissist that way is the way outa hell.

Lucifer was the first narcissist and that selfish spirit emanates from Satan and you're sick of it.

SEE HIM AS THE DEVIL [TO GET HIM OUT]
NO RESPECT FOR THE SAVAGE

See him as the devil and getting away from this emotional troublemaker is far less trouble.

All men are not that way. Get rid of him and focus on those who are decent and love ya' lady.

Get as far away from devil as you can then thank God you were rescued from heartbreak again.

Once the soul tie is gone you see him for what he is. Like Dorian Grey it's changed completely sis.

Soul ties paste a pretty face on that cad. Sin made him old and ugly but you couldn't see that.

Pinpoint the areas of narcissism and tell the world about em--like fickleness and game playin'.

Since no empathy or insight marks narcissism, he's not gonna change & you're better rid of him.

Have respect for the damage this person can do, the power he has and the impact for years too.

Don't give your breakup too much energy cuz remember he doesn't care anyway: enjoy the day.

MY ASIAN FEMALE BODY TYPE

THE COMMUNE IS A BAGASHIT

I've finally reached my Asian female body type which is 20 lbs under American and feels SO right.

For my Asian Female Body Type 94 pounds is fine for five foot three and running all of the time.

When I finally reached my ideal weight I felt so clean, pure, gentle and entirely true to God's will.

This is perfect but if unable to defend these views they'd put you in an eating disorder clinic too.

Any superfluity on the frame was an encumbrance and I was dulled by it. Body-mind complex, that's it.

On your fastarian proprioceptive journey you leave the world of food/drink and visit heaven see.

The most beautiful model in world was asked what she ate: she goes "right for the pies and cakes".

Give up on telling people WHAT to eat. Eat whatever you want the daily fast wipes it out see.

Three tacos every two days is perfect for me. This is how you beat inflation/get healthy see.

LITTLE GIRL OR MAGNETISM?

Give up the little girl act for the magnetic older woman and you'll see a big change in how they react.

He wanted to rough you up ok, make you jealous, put you in your place/get back at previous mates.

If a man hasn't made the transition from middle aged lecher to elderly gentleman, forget him.

When you transcend the soul tie you'll have an entirely different perception of that guy: UGLY!

THE COMMUNE IS A BAGASHIT

How fast love turns to hate! When it is a haunted house you date that's likely to be your fate.

Let SILENCE be your only defense. The minute you try to explain you've lost all your power sis.

Silence says it ALL. That's why it's golden and words can only fail: let his subconscious reveal.

Girl, you'll feel so much better when this nasty soul tie's gone: you're gonna be a queen soon hon'!

STOP STUFFING

Stop stuffing from the outside in. You're born with aesthetic knowledge and it's all WITHIN.

Long story short, you're had a life of serial relationships that were abusive, immoral and pointless.

Take a toke, listen to chill-out and enjoy the view even if a parking lot. Now wisdom will come up.

Watch as God pours burning coals on his head. That's the promise unless you choose to beg instead.

I don't care what a book you read said. Stop spilling your head, I heed what intuition reflects.

The undertow is so severe by the time a woman is mature she holds her head high for sure.

The new religious orthodoxy is a mixture of climate alarmism, socialism and transgenderism.

What good is a single shot when a 100 people mob your house? Need better weapons than foes.

COMMUNIST SPIRIT

CONFORMIST SYSTEMS
NO MORE MERITOCRACY
ANTI-WHITE VIOLATIONS
NEEDING APPROVAL OF CREEPS
CHEAP GRIFTERS EVERYWHERE
UNDERHANDED COMMIE SPIRIT
MEGHAN MARKLE: DEBUNKING TRADITION
NEVER COMPLAIN OR EXPLAIN
SOCIAL DEVICES AREN'T NICE
FAME DANGERS
COMMUNIST SPIRIT (TAUGHT TO SHARE)
GIVE AND THEY JUST WANT MORE
"SHARING" VS. PRIVATE PROPERTY
TRENDIES ARE PHONIES
TO SUCCEED, GET AWAY
WOMEN FIGHT THRU THE GRAPEVINE
FEAR OF COPS
CACKALING LAUGHTER
GOTTA LET YOU GO, CIAO
STAY AWAY FROM VIOLENCE-JUSTIFIERS
DIVERSITY IS A SHAKEDOWN
WOMEN ARE THE PROBLEM: MAD AT DAD
SAYING "NO" IS AN ACHIEVEMENT
LIBERALISM IS THE DEFAULT SETTING
LIBERALISM EVEN IN CHRISTIANS
GENDER CONFUSION READY FOR COMMUNISM
PORNOGRAPHY OK, TRUTH NOT-OK
DEBAUCHERY AND CEASELESS ORGIES
COMMIES ARE SHALLOW
FEMINISM DESTROYED OUR FREEDOM
DEMORALIZE FIRST, CONQUER SECOND

COMMUNIST SPIRIT

CRAZINESS AND HATE WILL ALWAYS DEFLATE
LIBERALISM EVEN IN THE CHURCHES
THE "OPPRESSED" ARE "VIRTUOUS"
JESUS HATED HYPOCRISY THE MOST
LIBERALS EXPLODE AS THEY LOSE
THE NARRATIVE: CUT IT LOOSE WITH NON-REPLY
TRUTH AND RIGHTEOUSNESS TRANSCENDS FAMILY
THE RELIGIOUS VIRTUE-SIGNALERS
SPIRIT OF JUSTICE OR LOVING THE DEVIL
EVERYTHING IS ABOUT RACE OR GENDER
THE YOUTH ARM OF THE DEMOCRATS
LET RIGHT DIVIDE FROM FALSE, NOW!
DIG IN, A CIVIL WAR'S COMING
ANTI-GLOBALISM IS BURGEONING
SOCIALISM APPEALS TO THE DUMB
WHITE GENOCIDE: BRED OUT OF EXISTENCE
ISOLATE TO AVOID DEMOGRAPHIC DESSTRUCTION
LIBERALS LOVE INVADERS AS VOTERS
DOCILE DEPENDENT WELFARE SLAVES
SOCIALIST COMMUNIST GLOBALIST
RUSSIAN YOUTH THE MOST PATRIOTIC
BUT WHITES DO IT TOO: NOT TRUE
NEVER A MENTION OF WHITE RACISM
SOCIALISM IS ALWAYS AUTHORITARIAN
AGEISM IS WORSE THAN RACISM
HIX POLITIX IS TRAGIC
GUESS I'M A WRITER
CONTENT CREATORS
FINAL FRUITARIANISM
ROLLING 48 [EAT EVERY OTHER DAY]

COMMUNIST SPIRIT

They're Mean Meddlers Too

People are nice when you're popular or rich but if you fall way down you're alone in a ditch.

CONFORMIST SYSTEMS

God must've known if you put a unique person in a conformist system there'd be problems.

Overcoming conformist systems to do your own thing is the battle for individuation of kings.

They kept wanting me to be part of the group and I'd keep escaping wanting ONLY to work.

First signs of lost freedom: first and second amendments, losing speech and our guns.

Few are aware of how race and gender pandering has undermined the culture and everything.

All institutions/schools are racist, giving preference to blacks and other minorities when hiring.

Since youth are increasingly exposed to identity politics/victimology it's a race war coming.

As long as implicit BIAS remains the ONLY explanation for success DISPARITIES, the left wins.

Though MLK wanted colorblind meritocracy it's near impossible to resume it unfortunately.

You can no longer count on the builders of bridges to be chosen by merit--don't ever bet on it.

THE COMMUNIST SPIRIT

NO MORE MERITOCRACY

Bridge builders/doctors not chosen for excellence but the color of their skin: how dangerous!

Colorblind meritorious achievements are shredded totally under the Biden administration.

Their new thing: teaching equality is racism, treating everyone the same is oppression.

Phrases like "dismantling whiteness and never allowing it to re-assert itself" makes me paranoid.

Taught in all schools now: the Pedagogy of the Oppressed, in racialized language and Marxist.

Equality is colorblindness/equal protection under the law. "Equity" as they mean it isn't at all.

Equity is: Active discrimination to rectify any racial disparities real or imagined in movies.

ANTI-WHITE VIOLATIONS

This anti-white trend in ALL institutions is a violation of the Civil Rights Act and the constitution.

The last defenders of Americana meritocracy are Asians on the west coast, academics most.

"Ethno-mathematics" says focus on finding the right answer [2 + 2 = 4] is white supremacist.

Changing standards is the soft bigotry of lowered expectations and students aren't dumb.

It is extremely common now that: teachers condemn conservatives and praise democrats.

THE COMMUNIST SPIRIT

What they are teaching innocence: ANY incarceration of blacks is an act of violence.

Disproportionate arguments are lazy because you just show disparities but not tell em why see.

Equity is: Active discrimination to rectify any racial disparities real or imagined in movies.

Much shame & guilt is a mal-adaptation to a blaming shaming liberal cuz that's how they play,

How to handle the millions of child migrants: Teach em all CIVICS and make em conservatives.

To the feminists: Yah men are bad but women are so much worse due to social hypnosis.

All I can do is write about the social neurosis and the escape cuz that was the entire landscape.

NEEDING APPROVAL OF CREEPS

You're still sore over the disapproval of people who can't lick your boots they're so evil?

It's called the Fallen Hero Syndrome: It's your own friends who kill you on the way down.

Biden spent 86 million [of your money man] to put illegal aliens in nice hotels: insane.

Unwittingly I let her hook-up on the land but when I said "no guests" she gossiped I was bad.

Every time I took someone in I wished I hadn't but dogs and cats are grateful and compliant.

They're a dumbed down mutual admiration society so phony it isn't funny: shun em completely.

THE COMMUNIST SPIRIT

Americana: you work, you eat. It's the opposite to the communist spirit of justified cheat.

Communist spirit is everywhere: you have two, I have none, give me one--regardless of merit.

The Borrowers are a subset of the communist spirit and you've had it--see it, reject it.

Work for what you get, keep it. You worked for home, they didn't--so don't let em move in kid.

You worked hard for those things. Don't lend em out to users who see em and start to think.

They come into your house, all carefully laid out with beauty, and they want some of it honey.

CHEAP GRIFTERS EVERYWHERE

Don't have these cheap grifters in your life any more. Cut the past if it means these characters.

Respect you, respect your things, respect your privacy and property--that's an American honey.

An introvert has just as much right to live as an extrovert but still the social world yells.

It wasn't due to skin color that they rejected her but leftist ideals, virtue signaling and poor character.

If not a overt racist you're a covert racist which cannot be seen, proven nor disproven just assumed.

It's a weaponized kindness they use to deflect all criticism--it's a lethal contradiction.

Mental illness hits like physical illness does. There were years I wasn't my mostess, I was a dud.

THE COMMUNIST SPIRIT

Constant comments on how your selfies look. Don't you get sick of shallow--where's your content?

Instead of remorsing over all your sins why not chalk the whole era up to mental illness? Saves time

Sins are mental illness. For every sin there's a seed of compensation in the present = that is it.

Mentally illness is keeping company with demons unawares/it's scary looking back I declare.

I never witnessed such narcissism as all your selfies. But if an older model it's ok see.

UNDERHANDED COMMIE SPIRIT

One is mentally ill due to false dogma from schools, social hebephrenia, drugs, fornication, food.

If expressing your opinion and famous you've had it--it's hazardous cuz they'll come to your house.

They'll find your address, put the GPS in a phone and come right to your door.

It's not safe to talk but only to write in abstruse political poetry in short quips on contradiction.

They'll come to your house with an army, break your windows and kill your dogs. Need a WALL.

Flood us with illegals/gangs and take our guns. Thanks a lot democrats, destroyers for bucks.

If you're white you must hate yourself and promote all other races, religions and differences.

Typical work place of obsequiousness, extreme anxiety, blind obeisance, suppression of thought.

THE COMMUNIST SPIRIT

In Western capitalism work was divine worship and success indicated God's approval of it.

Jezebel uses people--flying monkeys--to do her dirty work, like if she's jealous of another girl.

If you don't use social skills you lose em--that's ok I haven't said 2 words in two years they say.

When I leave this earth i leave you too--it's all left behind so why should I bother now, that's my mind.

If I fall head over heels in love I fall over a cliff too so I fight against this tendency as should you.

MEGHAN MARKLE: DEBUNKING TRADITION

Never complain, never explain. The royal edict makes sense to never be looked down on again.

Who can blame Meghan, the press is a loose cannon and to lose all control like that is aggravatin'

Complain--if you're rich--and they hate you. Explain and it's like you're kissing UP like you have to.

The system is unforgiving/in strife so the answer for scapegoats is just move and live a good life.

Move, live a good life and let em talk all they want. You're just a name at this point and they've lost.

It doesn't matter what they say, you're far away. Live a good life and Jesus has the past erased.

They were jealous of me so no matter what I said it was viewed as ungrateful cuz they're fullabull.

The better you are the more triggering of deep lunacies so you gotta escape that matrix see.

THE COMMUNIST SPIRIT

NEVER COMPLAIN OR EXPLAIN

When they accuse you, don't explain. I know it's your tendency but it makes you inferior, inane.

When you're rich, never complain. They're already so jealous it just makes them more insane.

Yes I always come out on top. They're never gonna put me down again like the Dunning-Kruger block.

When dumbasses are in control you're in big trouble. You don't want cruel men over the lovable.

The rich or royal can still be rigid thinkers and novelty will be seen as inferior causing heartbreak dear.

Meghan's sister changed name back to Markle only after she started dating Harry: social psychology.

Not saying I'm for Meghan, she's a lost leftist always virtue-signaling about liberal positions.

Prohibited: One can be rich and privileged and still experience emotional or mental illness.

SOCIAL DEVICES AREN'T NICE

Being rich doesn't inoculate you from the pain of social devices based on jealousy and hate.

Even knowing it's false, they'll go along with the narrative because they don't like her, that's all.

One can be very rich and famous and still suffer mental illness but they'll hate her if she confesses.

It's a matter of what daily negativity does to your personal psyche tho' you can see right thru it see.

THE COMMUNIST SPIRIT

Like any scapegoat in any system she had a nonstop barrage of negative press that's not true.

Bible says it's a wide path to hell and a narrow one to heaven so how is the majority right on?

They had me all wrong based on social-neurotic grounds and it made me mad inside/in the dumps.

By far the biggest Dunning-Kruger effect is being alone if you're smart. Know this from the start.

Meghan's reaction to social rigidity was contumacy because she's used to independence see.

If you're not overtly racist they'll get you on "covert" racism which is invisible: not seen nor heard.

Facts don't matter it's their "experience" mattering more. That's the line causing confusion galore.

The youth go with Meghan & Harry, the oldsters go with the royal family--it's generational honey.

Liberalism is contumacious so of course leftists in America will be against royalty: facts.

Thankfully old age doesn't last very long. Soon you're dead and youth will have to come along.

FAME DANGERS

If fame brings death threats and need for guards who would need it desperately/be so unaware.

They loved Meghan at first then she started her leftist crap and they turned-- how is this racist sir?

Never back into your future by always looking backwards. Your time has come, be mature, go forwards.

THE COMMUNIST SPIRIT

If you start a fast and then eat, don't binge--a partial fast can work very well in healing even lungs.

It was horrible. He was Jolly Jimmy to the world and a monster sadist to his wife. Al-Anon

You're fruitarian--there is hope now. It's all over, the whole mess from culture foods: wow.

It's not about money or selling books--get offa that thing--it's about getting it out while I could.

Work is the way to buttress your inflated view of yourself, to prove the reason for your grandiosity.

WHEN WORK IS A PLEASURE

When work is a pleasure, life is a joy. When work is a duty, life is slavery. Maxim Gorky

The baby's skin color was inquired by a liberal wanting him black enough to be multi-cultural.

It'd be like someone worked for you/you were good to them and later they played the victim.

Those gossiping about me were steeped in sex sins acceptable to liberals and condoned.

You were a victim/sitting duck but now you're behind a gate with a lock, that's the whole think doc.

It is very minimizing to me psychologically when I say something and you deflect/look away.

The communist spirit has wrecked millions of lives from toddlers on: forced to share/LIES.

THE COMMUNIST SPIRIT (TAUGHT TO SHARE)

THE COMMUNIST SPIRIT

People take advantage of a good heart and it's heartbreaking to let em go but you must for a new start.

Communist spirit: "You have three, I have none so give me one".

When you encounter the communist spirit run the other way or quickly put up your boundaries.

Covetousness--acquisitiveness--is a common emotion so stop giving away your possessions.

The ability to say NO without feeling selfish is about boundaries so start practicing with this.

People have to respect you but also your things. It's not theirs but the communist spirit rings.

So you get nice things, can you keep em? A fool is easily separated from money or possessions.

Be cautious of the sucking spirit that wants to take things from you so that it can be theirs.

The successful, intelligent, informed mavericks and trailblazers all know this new authoritarianism.

Leech defined: Sticky fingers, sucking spirit.

Communist spirit: if you have three and I have one you *owe* me one: liberals are terrible/no fun.

When one gives you something never ask for more or you'll never see em again if they're mature.

Give gifts to an evil person and he just wants more and this is his karma: you shut the door.

Giving to them gives em the idea to hit you up for more--it was the trigger for all you abhor.

Giving acts as a trigger as they ask for more cuz it's a new idea they never thought of before.

THE COMMUNIST SPIRIT

GIVE AND THEY JUST WANT MORE

If you give em something and they ask for more they've poor character and you know it for sure.

I thought it was isolated incidents of theft but it's a whole generation with spirt of communists.

It doesn't matter that it was just a pencil it's still not theirs and respect for private property is rare.

You're never allowed to store in quantity, the liberals want it and they deserve it is their fantasy.

Just cuz they demand it doesn't mean you have to give it. People eye your things and want it.

With the house a leaky boat cuz you lend to a toad it's like a sucking spirit/you're outa control.

They saw it and they want it, period. That's the child in adults and we're darn sick of it.

Le Femme and the Communist Spirit: my next book about this school-bred mentality: fear it.

When that sucking spirit wants what you own that's when your house becomes a leaky boat.

If your friends are the borrowers your house is like a leaking boat and hey man, you're outa control.

Don't let people take things from your house. Show them where to get it on their own, the louse.

When people ask to borrow do you feel uncomfortable? Do you give in to be "nice" to the rabble?

THE BORROWERS: "SHARING" VS. PRIVATE PROPERTY

THE COMMUNIST SPIRIT

Everything you bought was cuz you wanted it. Stop lending it cuz that's the last you'll see of it.

Those things are there because you wanted them, where do they get off upsetting your plans?

It has nothing to do with you being "selfish" so get offa that thing--they just saw you coming.

She's not your friend but your foe--because of her your house is unsecured/a leaky boat.

She took advantage and I'm a dam pushover. A recluse doesn't know any better but it's still a fetter.

Sucking spirit grabs on then bleeds you.

The guts of globalism is about being heartless, soulless, and using other people, seen as "strength".

Since everyone wants a piece of me I gotta have him betwixt me and thee.

Leech, sucking spirit = leaky boat/fear it.

1400 years this religion has created giant armies of inbred insane people resulting in deformities/evil.

Sucking spirit: grab on, bleed out.

When someone gives you something never ask for more lest you lose them & your future for sure.

Giving to them is the trigger to ask for more then they're out the door and what a relief--you soar.

You give, they want more. Another way of saying: give em an inch and they take a mile, clear?

Total domestication phase: half the country's on the dole.

THE COMMUNIST SPIRIT

People filled with the devil due to sin make mistakes, overreach and bring themselves down.

TRENDIES ARE PHONIES

Geniuses are not into current trends except recovering from the emotional/mental trauma of them.

Being smart isn't going along with trends. Give up this white guilt thing, stay mentally stable friends.

Can't you see you're just parroting thru fear? It's embarrassing dear, I thought you were smarter.

It's insane how women get divorced to their obvious detriment. Loyalty to an idea but dying quick.

By you going along with these current trends I see you're a dummy and I never knew you, a fake friend.

When I hear you using buzz words and current phrases it makes me sick, here I thought you were hip.

If you're a slave to your fans [having to go along] that's not strength. Say the truth in boldness, this stinks!

They get divorced like it's just another option. But it's the most serious thing, the biggest decision, amen.

A current trend [something never thought of yesterday] you see as gospel truth, how embarrassing.

Why would you cowtow and bow before these people? Your appeasing weakness is so dam evil.

"I can't live with that demon in the house. Home is everything to me and now it's sullied." Lady

TO SUCCEED, GET AWAY

THE COMMUNIST SPIRIT

If you stay in the relationship the psychological wounds from the narcissist become increasingly serious.

Show self-love by not going back to a channel that hurt you. Always say "NO" and turn from the world.

There are decades when nothing happens and there are weeks when decades happen. V. I. Lenin

"Just following orders" yes but if taking orders from Deep State it's called "betrayal"--then executioners.

A genius is sensitive to changes. Thus they adapt earlier and create amazing discoveries and inventions.

You were a clog in the line and then the writing became all about suffering. Writers need solitude, truly.

It's you coming up with things without an integrating theory: a matrix/paradigm or central worldview.

I feel so much better out of your web. That was a sticky situation and I'm lucky I overcame you bud.

WOMEN FIGHT THRU THE GRAPEVINE

Women: I knew you were gossiping about me but never confronted you since you'd just do it more, see?

Women fight with their mouths thru a grapevine. How many can suffer alone without calling to whine?

They get all their friends against you. They don't even have to be angry, it's just their DNA to make you blue.

She did so many vicious things it's just easier to forgive her--clean slate--rather than giving into hate.

Once married they're ashamed all the things they did when you were defenseless: that's the herd Miss.

THE COMMUNIST SPIRIT

There are still many sweet little ladies but they're dying out. Along with this few are taught to keep house.

It's up to the female to put brakes on sexually but modern women are like the men were viewed to be.

FEAR OF COPS

The moral of the story which there's no doubt: If you burn enough buildings you get what you want.

If you bow to the mob you get more mobs. Jared Taylor

My real fear of cops began when under Obama they were militarized suddenly and **TERRIFYINGLY.**

Though I moved to the desert for peace and solitude, by four mean cops it was ruled so I isolated/withdrew.

Obama geared up the cops with scary looking military equipment so how could we **NOT** fear them?

One cop hung out with Liquor Store Linda getting the daily scoop. When you think about it, **SHE** ruled.

Before Obama the cops were good ol' chaps but then he geared em up to persecute patriots/dissidents.

Whoever Liquor Store Linda had a beef with she'd share with the cops "visiting" her [disappearances].

That's just a little view of Hix Politix in small desert towns where we're all hot, hemmed in and pissed.

The main cop went to the most popular [false] church and everyone wanted to be his friend, of course.

We don't have cops here but then we don't need em, we're all stable Christians just into our own homes.

THE COMMUNIST SPIRIT

As Tom Jefferson said, these principals only work for a **MORAL** people, you must have that first.

No hanky panky with the neighbor's wife cuz we're all into our own homes not promiscuous socializing.

CACKALING LAUGHTER

Cheese cake smiles: why? It looks so fake it's much more elegant to just be yourself and not smile at all.

Liberals are entirely too social and it's boring as hell. They fake laugh over nothing, it's scary and unreal.

Fake laugh: what's so funny? They're always yelling with loud raucous laughter about actually nothing.

It's now excruciatingly boring, an anachronism from another era when I obviously felt so lowly.

Jocularity, raucous laughter sounds like cackling flames on an open fire. Her loud shrieks grit my nerves!

Liberals laugh **LOUDLY** about nothing cuz their main thing is getting **ATTENTION** in a social generation.

Laughter--always gotta interject it after saying anything. People used to be serious/handsome/pretty.

Nothing scarier than laughter from nowhere. The devilish laugh as they stab you in that back, beware.

Smiling like a Cheshire Cat doesn't make you friendly. Showing teeth is a sign of aggression in reality.

GOTTA LET YOU GO, CAIO

I gotta let you go so I can do my own thing unobstructed by what you think. Sorry but this is destiny.

THE COMMUNIST SPIRIT

You must compartmentalize it to live with it. Tuck it away, sweep under the rug, distract/try to forget it.

I can't go there anymore because you love to hurt me, that's who you are.

You've become excruciatingly boring/irrelevant to me. No juice, a waste of time, nothing interesting, bye.

Though you're younger you seem like a dirty old man to me. Sorry I guess I'll always feel like a teen.

I'm leery of anyone with power over me. Government, groups, militarized cops or a gossiping old lady.

I've reached a point where I gotta be on my own. What you think or anyone else cannot be my concern.

I'm gonna die sooner not later so why waste time on this? It's another dimension I don't care for/resist.

Only through my words do I know myself. Interviews are just too close, it's the words that come first.

I won't compete with your narc harem. It's so degrading I'd rather stay home with pets and enjoy em.

I still want you, it's you I want but if I can't have you I'll still have a ball every day on earth, that's all.

STAY AWAY FROM VIOLENCE-JUSTIFIERS

Stay away from an entire generation brainwashed to justify violence with any little disagreement.

Learning about the Holocaust and Hitler keeps things in proper perspective: that life is very serious.

Once you learn what can happen you proceed with caution not do outrageous things bringing your end son.

THE COMMUNIST SPIRIT

Third parties add games, ill fames, nondiscernment [saying it's all the same] and they're boring--no way.

Once you know how fast they can turn you don't act that way anymore--a giant step to success, I declare.

Much misbehavior is due to demons from sin and weakness. A broken hedge, disorder/a mess.

DIVERSITY IS A SHAKEDOWN

Diversity is a shakedown: shut up white people and pay up.

Grow government, get rid of middle class, transfer money offshore, make us dependent and poor.

You got rid of God but now you've got the state which is much worse than God. Stefan Molyneux

In general, virtue increases as intelligence increases--then there's the bell curve of the vicious.

The New Right is about loyalty to one's own people (white Europeans) tho' that's all seen as evil.

Welfare is merely the method of transforming the market economy step by step into socialism.

It is difficult to free fools from the chains they revere. Voltaire

If you control the person's healthcare you control the person. Lenin

If socialists understood economics, they wouldn't be socialists. Frederick Von Hayek

Real Indians want local politics, fake Indians (Liz Warren) want centralized gov/a communist.

Demise of the left is the demise of global politics: a one-world cosmology and we're sick of it.

THE COMMUNIST SPIRIT

Migrants and leftists flock to the cities and I'm glad of that--stay away from the country, please!

Is it true the less we have in common the stronger we are?

No socialism in America as the poor feel like temporarily embarrassed millionaires. John Steinbeck

WOMEN ARE THE PROBLEM: MAD AT DAD

As a social psychologist the cultural mental illness is my business.

I'm mad at women for their virtue signaling calling it politics and their loving big gov/open borders.

Children love having mother and father together. It's paradise on earth, birds of feather.

Hedonism came along and said to hell with it all just enjoy thyself: societal decay/family collapse.

Sex Ed is nothing but hardcore porn, a national disgrace as they impose this crap on five year olds.

Evil means to destroy the man by telling women he's vermin and paying them to leave em.

All men are horrible so if you say you're a victim you're in the cool club.

The laws must be changed: no more false accusations of child molestation in courts for leverage.

Educating the mind without educating the heart is no education at all. Aristotle

The old hippie called "Cher", the aging pop star, popped off about Trump calling him a cancer.

Enlightenment is not getting happier but the crumbling away of untruth--seeing through pretense.

THE COMMUNIST SPIRIT

Obama-led drone strikes killed innocent 90% of the time but she still loves this communist slime.

SAYING "NO" IS AN ACHIEVEMENT

The people who don't know anything will never say "no" to anything. Mark Passio

I will call you "hate speech" if I hate the fact I can't argue back.

Domesticate us so we can't defend or feed ourselves, so they take control when it all goes to hell.

They didn't have fathers so were accosted/gave into young boys and it's been that way since.

Without fathers they're always in withdrawal, symptoms: yelling, pleading, threatening, crying.

When you swim in muddy waters get a little mud on you and most from blue states have a little P-U.

Women are excited by men who are skeptical of their value. Stefan Molyneux

Obama/Hillary are literal demons (smell bad) but the selfish don't care, can you imagine that?

Doctrines of demons, sanctuary of devils: It's happening folks, the false church slippery slope.

Thank God sexuality is diminishing for me, it's like casting out a demon. – Socrates in his 70's.

Education is the kindling of a flame, not the filling of a vessel. Socrates

LIBERALISM IS THE DEFAULT SETTING

The brain is an organ damaged by education.

If you hate Trump you can do whatever you want spnd be totally forgiven/part of the club.

THE COMMUNIST SPIRIT

University liberals are given everything because they signed onto the globalist program/fiends.

We're in the grip of a fascistic leftist theocracy stifling, squelching, attacking anti-dogmatists.

Civilization ceases to exist when debate and reason is no longer allowed. Stefan Molyneux

Our commitment to free speech means the left must impose itself thru aggression, ostracism, rejection.

Without facts on their side they all become verbal abusers: slander is the tool of losers. Socrates

Government is the great fiction thru which everyone seeks to live at the expense of everyone else.

Politicians and diapers must be changed often and for the same reason. Mark Twain

Donald loves Kanye West so how could he be a racist?

Trump has dragon energy: creative, disruptive energy. Shaking things up, golden age of vitality.

Kanye West should reject all who rejected him for loving Trump. Bet they're all women, huh.

Two ways to be fooled: believe what is not true or refuse to believe what is true. Soren Kierkegaard

Even tho' they were weak/mind controlled we have still turned us against them, tho' forgiven.

The hottest love has the coldest end. Socrates

Women aren't smart enough to process information running counter to emotional preferences?

THE COMMUNIST SPIRIT

I do so love Donald Trump. Kanye West

NRA raking in millions as a backlash against vermin so go ahead and protest more is comin'.

Just cuz you got em to go along with you doesn't make it right, good, intelligent or out of sight.

You can make people do what you want, I'll grant you that. It's a real talent but you're still a brat.

LIBERALISM EVEN IN CHRISTIANS

Christians going left in the American schism: letting in refugees and battling nonexistent racism.

In healthy times, great nations are conscious of their past and anxious to pass on what has been won.

Self-hatred is implanted in your kids by vicious crybaby ideologues, a toxic environment.

In the world of secular liberalism you can abort your kids, you just can't spank em.

Stop letting mental pipsqueaks tell you what to think.

Secular Modernity is the globalist's cramdown and it's incomprehensibly evil, dirty and wrong.

Statistically women vote for open borders and bigger government so *they* are the problem!

Because they lead with their heart (a good start) they can't see the bigger picture/not real smart.

Caring about the welfare of animals is not a leftist but a humanist position.

Rosanne: All about economics not about 2016 cultural revolution—she missed that we're all sick of this.

THE COMMUNIST SPIRIT

Saying it's about economics is downplaying the immorality and sick invasion of feminism in politics.

GENDER CONFUSION READY FOR COMMUNISM

Roseanne reflected Hollywood cramdown saying you "can't raise kids in traditional gender roles".

Trump is a cultural warrior elected due to blowback from gender role confusion/return to facts.

New Normal: Era of the Political Right.

Blowback: unintended consequences of brainwash. Cramdown: media inculcation by ideologues.

It is not healthy to avoid reinforcing gender roles or to produce gender confusion in children.

Every single culture through time has gender-based dress, so boys become men to defend us.

The liberals contradict saying "clothes don't make a difference" so why put our boys in a dress?

The bible is very strict against cross dressing.

Shift from secular, modernist, transcultural liberal human rights paradigm to reality: yours and mine.

Civic nationalism: Whether black or white we were proud citizens of a country achieving so much.

Americana is a culture and strong tradition held together by common religious commitments.

Donald Trump ratings are up at 51% despite overwhelmingly negative (95%) media coverage.

How I know all: I had to learn to deal with juvenile pre-prison criminals to learn about liberals.

THE COMMUNIST SPIRIT

I didn't have to go to prison to learn it I got a big dose of invading liberal thieves in Borrego Springs.

Loving liberals invaded me, brought all their friends to steal from me then evaded all responsibility.

See your foes as the scum bags they really are to return to the pleasure of knowing you're right, a star.

PORNOGRAPHY OK, TRUTH NOT-OK

Pornography: broken families, loose relationships, malleable minds and shattered societies.

Pornography shrinks frontal part of the brain (will power/moral compass) so he can't refrain.

Millennials don't wanna be with a human being cuz it's a 7 when a 10 {porn} releases dopamine.

Warning: People are loyal only in times of stability but weakness is attacked so keep your head up, ok?

Even 9 month old babies prefer toys specific to their gender. Biologically boys are defenders.

Even male monkey babies wanna play with trucks not dolls, ok?

Denialism--denying facts due to idealism--is such a huge study you can even get a Ph.D. in it.

Liberals think that if we don't end up the same, injustice is happening and the whites are to blame.

If you have a white boy be mindful of his school. Things have changed beyond recognition, uncool.

The feminist teachers indoctrinate through hysteria and it's the most serious thing in America.

THE COMMUNIST SPIRIT

If a child is told he is bad for his race it's so destructive it'll take years to undo, yet you say it.

I hate liberalism and wish we could have worthy debates but why do they always have to escape?

You want him to be all he can be so stop nagging at he.

One-ist cosmology: so inveterate, obdurate and completely laid out they think it makes em free.

DEBAUCHERY AND CEASELESS ORGIES

Debauchery, ceaseless orgy is human history.

Obama killed the economy then started race wars: total abuse of power yet libs love him more.

They want us without identity, to be malleable. Not a race, nation, religion, not even a gender.

If you don't have an identity it's very easy for cultural Marxists to give you one and it's nasty.

They overplayed it when we went from accepting queers to men in the bathroom marked "hers".

Every animal has self-defense and Jesus said if your enemy has a sword, get a better one fast.

Make yourself sheep and the wolves will eat you. Mark Twain

Equality of opportunity is freedom, equality of outcome is tyranny.

University: Blacks are never guilty of racism/whites are always guilty of racism, it's unconscious.

Machiavelli: How the haves keep power. Saul Alinsky: How the have-nots can take it away.

THE COMMUNIST SPIRIT

Mr. or Mrs. Superior give you sermons on how to conform to them and it's always virtue signaling.

He tortured us for eight years ending with the whole world hating us and it's *him* you miss?

COMMIES ARE SHALLOW

College professor means: dumbness, abuse of power and mediocrity.

Why are women so stupid/shallow? They weren't born that way, just want each other's approval.

Men don't support the world for other men or "patriarchy" but for women and children, you and me.

Say the truth and offend everyone big time or stay quiet and warp your soul: think on this/decide.

Biggest myth: If we outlaw guns they won't be plentiful. But with prohibition they drank to their fill.

Feminists lie about campus rape culture, gender pay gap and the patriarchy—it's all malarkey.

The 2nd amendment is for defense against criminal gov (rare) but mostly lunatic mobs creating terror.

We live in a republic which prevents the MOB from taking over our individual rights or love of God.

We need guns to protect against lunatic mobs for the left is most virulent and objection's not allowed.

Their idea of Christianity is virtue signaling on trendy topics, the ones most people agree with.

Whenever someone says "We're all God" or "all churches are the same" escape to where you came.

THE COMMUNIST SPIRIT

Their false religion compels them to push the envelope downstream until their total destruction.

Leftists dismiss religion as mental illness.

Other religions treat women like vermin but Christian men treat em like gold until wrecked by feminism.

Women were always rewarded the kids but now (with decay) judge gives em to a homosexual to raise.

FEMINISM DESTROYED OUR FREEDOM

Our women enjoyed great liberty/freedom until feminism destroyed those privileges, long gone.

Men used to break their neck to open a door for a lady, now that's all gone due to feminism: shady.

"Male and female created He them" and that division is clear all thru scripture but not in Babylon.

Couple decades back they woulda bashed the male trash going into women's bathroom like that.

America's real men never tolerated this crap back then. How we long for those days back again!

And the same be said for some of you but now you're washed and changed as filthy sin's gone too.

The Bible makes every society happier and better so the devilish elites want it banned forever.

Why don't most churches ever talk about sin? Having no power they ignore it/throw in trash bin.

Our children are raised up right then slowly turn away as they're sucked into lies/deception every day.

THE COMMUNIST SPIRIT

Nothing has any meaning except as it relates to Him, and that's how a Christian is a Christian.

YouTube employees could be shot by someone banned by them as they're in a gun free zone.

Trump was elected against Hollywood cramdown of things like gender roles which Roseanne reflects too.

DEMORALIZE FIRST, CONQUER SECOND

In public and even church life, traditional morality grounded in Christianity has been discarded.

You brought all your friends to our house and didn't think about our loss of privacy one bit--twit!

Let the far right be the new consensus, the new normal.

"Far right" was a pejorative term but now we're not just a margin we're the mainstream, growin'.

Threat to localized identity markers = reversion to national symbols to resist global invaders.

The new conservative age is literally transforming the entire world.

Never taught how to act they were brought up in a jungle in fact so I say stay away/never go back.

There is nothing more intolerant than secular liberalism.

The resurgence of nationalism entails a process of re-traditionalization.

Religion's common enemies are secular liberalism and jihadist terrorism.

Anti-social behavior is a trait of intelligence in a world full of conformists. Nikola Tesla

UK youth perturbed with older generations for voting Brexit--that's how outa touch and globalist.

THE COMMUNIST SPIRIT

If pedophilic all it takes is one glance/nod and that's it. Nothing discussed it's like an animal lit.

CRAZINESS AND HATE WILL ALWAYS DEFLATE

Never argue with teens, support them in craziness cuz it will bring our win and they'll deflate.

Liberals: fat-acceptance is hitched to thin privilege.

They only want to return to their virtue-signaling and slamming of non-liberal realists.

Why is he not working--is he looking at pornography? Cuz that stunts their growth completely.

It's a battle of narratives. If it's done by social utilities we're on a fast track to hell for you and me.

Ideology linked to color: Non-whites wanna take the guns and constitution doesn't matter.

Help him to be all he can be not by scolding and yelling but leading, encouraging, being.

Libs don't want people around with reason/evidence on their side as it causes emotional freakouts.

If he has out-group preferences the home is a mess.

LIBERALISM EVEN IN THE CHURCHES

We had to put up with your guy for eight years so now you know how it feels but your creepy antics are surreal.

Crazy paid leftist professors made em crazy and violent losers. Lunatic mobs are now running us, sir.

Democrats want to replace citizens with newly amnestied voters, not caring what your wants are.

THE COMMUNIST SPIRIT

In America white is bad/minorities are virtuous so you'd never have an Indian say he's white of course.

Obama trip: In all movies and cartoons whites are portrayed as idiots and non-whites as cool and hip.

THE "OPPRESSED" ARE "VIRTUOUS"

People who are labeled "oppressed" have a patina of virtuousness, increasing their dating chances.

The nice man said "I stand at the flag, I kneel at the cross" then he lost his job.

To deflect from their deficiencies the left clings to some moral high ground but it's all made up and silly.

ALL IS ONE is the shove down since kindergarten.

Vegans are SJWs and hate dogs. They want em shafted like meat animals so it's all "equal".

The most dangerous and horrible goal is EQUAL OUTCOMES. Nothing spells disaster/tyranny more, in sum.

We have a serious problem with mass mental illness in this country. Like calling judges gang rapist, crazy.

Obama's an example: Shiny surface, glib as heck but a shyster as disappointing as a bad check.

Professors dividing families/marriages with this crap. We hardly recognize kids when they come back.

Oh my, can it get any worse? "There is no limit to worse". Jordan Peterson

What offends can't be defined so it's just a way to complete control of our suckered minds.

Is it any wonder she'd be 01% Indian than 99% white, with the benefits given to minorities no matter what?

THE COMMUNIST SPIRIT

You're solitary (intellectual) but they're an echo chamber (social social) so the majority wins? Hell no!

Nazism was socialist. Anytime tyranny prevails you see this: saying they're "good" then turning murderous.

Avoided my generation cuz it stank and stinks worse today. Seek higher and older with something to say.

JESUS HATED HYPOCRISY THE MOST

Jesus hated hypocrisy the most. Pharisees were concerned with clean cups but inside all morals were lost.

Get ready for a huge red wave backlash--count on a landslide--but there may be some casualties besides.

They either don't know history or just don't want to admit it, justifying morally where they're at.

White men freed the slaves. For that cause they lost their limbs and lives and you say America is racist?

White men freed the slaves. Slavery was a fact throughout the world but whites ended it in America, ok?

If the blacks wake up it's over for the democratic party. They depend on them staying dumb, truly.

Anyone standing for good will be attacked, but that's all right: be brave and the Lord will have your back.

Blacks are the worst enemy of black conservatives--even in their own family called Uncle Tom, sellout.

The entire liberal world has turned against ya Kanye but it's all ok cuz the Great White Hope loves ya.

White men freed the slaves. Slavery was everywhere, owned by blacks--far more cruel than whites/FACT.

THE COMMUNIST SPIRIT

If you're black you're expected to be democrat. If you aren't watch out as your brothers will attack.

Barrack Obama was the worst president we've had in history. He emptied the prisons for the votes, truly.

LIBERALS EXPLODE AS THEY LOSE

Children of the Lie reacting like someone poured water on a witch--they've lost control and in a ditch.

If you allow the wrong people to get into office or your house things can change real fast: heed message.

Disgusting (disappointed) democrats want to break up the family and open up the borders/full amnesty.

They're not trying to make a political point that is cogent but make their enemies cower in fear, broken.

Language-loading: managing our thoughts to go in a certain direction and that's why you thought em.

In the democrat party you must have a victim story so you can lead the charge like the great in history.

If reviews make you mad, don't read the reviews--a dumbed down generation seeks to give you the blues.

What you say liberals call crazy cuz they've learned by rote/can't fit you into that public school matrix.

The creative genius NOVELTY in your utterances/writings will always be called CRAZY in the liberal matrix.

Voters are tuning out hype, smarter than media thinks they are--as usual. They just want the issues.

Minority benefits are why people would rather be 001.% American Indian rather than 99% white.

THE COMMUNIST SPIRIT

One person from Norway is not a minority--no, they are irrelevant as despicably white already.

Anyone who is not white (no matter background) is equal in their virtuousness due to white oppression?

How to explore higher dimensions and make discoveries: REJECT the herd, the social and current heresies.

THE NARRATIVE: CUT IT LOOSE WITH NON-REPLY

If you wanna be a genius discoverer you must cut it all loose: the current narrative or anything else.

As interesting as it all is you must STOP attending to this crap. Repeat and endless debates: scrap!

The situation changes every day and I know it's fascinating but you have bigger fish to fry/more to say.

Don't get hung up on stuff that is forgettable/soon obsolete. That's daily news of what we have to beat.

Deep State started in 70's so now hippies are well-entrenched in bureaucracies where the real trouble lies.

Donald Trump is our only bastion of defense against the radical left who would crush us given the chance.

What I had to go through to learn boundaries! I was a yes-person, when I said "NO" I felt so unloving/guilty.

They bothered me day and night. I finally got restraining orders then the town called me "anti-social"/a blight.

They'd conflate attendance to boring get-togethers as loyalty to God or sobriety--all is socially-driven.

Judges must now go through mandatory "unconscious bias" retraining-- meaning: brainwashing.

THE COMMUNIST SPIRIT

There is no proof of "unconscious bias" it's just a political weapon, so refuse to go to retraining sessions.

You're not misogynist or racist or homophobe so by going to retraining sessions you're admitting to it.

Biggest political heist of all times: they groomed O. perfectly for the job as closer of a 100 year plan.

If you were paid 65 million a year by Soros, would you tell the truth if you knew you would lose that?

TRUTH AND RIGHTEOUSNESS TRANSCENDS FAMILY

He took everything and you think it's all-ok just cuz he's family? Right and wrong come first baby.

The hippy's core value was sexual license so of course they want abortion on demand the despicable louses.

They've been so cut off from their destiny they're little barbarians, shallow roots adapting to ruffians.

Why are liberals unable to see this? Because liberalism is a mental illness.

If we lose this election we'll descend into hell, I can't even begin to tell.

"Trump hopes his supporters will kill journalists" means we live in two separate parallel news universes.

They're opinion leaders/gatekeepers of the status quo. They want us dumb to accept it all by rote.

While democrats produce mobs, republicans produce jobs. Donald Trump

Winning generals are always fighting the next war, loser generals are always fighting the last one.

Conservative means you wanna keep things the same.

THE COMMUNIST SPIRIT

Real men are conservative, republicans, strong in nature. Progressives are beta males who don't really care.

The LEFT will destroy you to get power and wealth. Do you know anyone like this, family or fellows?

Pelosi: We're so sick of her communist antics, we just can't help it--shut up and get outa here, hypocrite!

THE RELIGIOUS VIRTUE-SIGNALERS

The more religious the more virtue-signaling and that means befriending your enemies and calling it loving.

Globalist pawn and horrible woman Ms. Cortez rising up through the ranks of other democrat vermin.

Wow! Leftist insanity on display. This is how they think people so let it inoculate you.

Promises made, promises kept! What a relief after 8 years of that weasel dictator, how we wept!

We're sick of social justice racists "fightin' for the folks"

I overreacted to his porn but it's a sudden incursion of an evil spirit making me hate the day i was born.

Things happen and they don't know how to handle it cuz they don't have a savior so blame us instead.

They'll do anything to hold you back/block your success. They don't care what it took, you've had it.

GRIT, tenacity, sticking to something, overcoming--old virtues are now replaced with: are you a victim?

Liberal media gushing over democrat rockstars--just like with Obama they've been slobbering for years.

THE COMMUNIST SPIRIT

Ha ha. The average white person in America has TEN TIMES the native blood as Elizabeth Warren.

These animals are not like you. They will tear your arm off and gobble you up too.

A herd animal cannot change course on its own. That's why the ship of fools is on it's way--way down.

Democrats wanted a witchhunt which fizzled from lack of evidence. Again we see the chicanery of dunces.

A lone voice in the wilderness is not necessarily wrong. Ghandi

With the swearing in of Judge Kavanaugh the 70-year era of liberal rule has ended.

SPIRIT OF JUSTICE OR LOVING THE DEVIL

You don't love the Spirit of Justice, you love the devil. You love death, being replaced, dark angels.

Liberal judicial tyranny is over. Conservatives and the constitution will rule for a hundred years or more!

Calling someone "Nazi" is codespeak for anyone who disagrees.

Things can always get worse. There's no bottom to "worse": Trudeau's new budget--no "boys and girls".

More money, Trump: Freedom to be relieved of unnecessary drudgery, freedom to shop till we drop.

You judge people on their talent, wisdom and character--NOT identity politics like what color they are.

Democrats suffering their irrelevance. Or, should they be even more cool and go hard left like dunces?

The violent left isn't intellectual, these are party people: hacks, degenerates, misfits and drones.

THE COMMUNIST SPIRIT

Line between dangerous extremist and U.S. senator is being blurred on the left--they just can't get over it.

Loving left shows snarling, narcissistic blind rage. We should be happy about this since it seals their fate.

Intersectionality is the ruthless totem pole of victimhood. Culprit is always the same: white men/no good.

EVERYTHING IS ABOUT RACE OR GENDER

Everything is about race or gender cuz the liberal democrats must pit one group against another.

The tolerant left entered my house, broke all the windows and tore the phone out cuz I wanted Kavanaugh.

Conservatives are better looking from their great lives which libs see as "ethical blind spot--can't empathize".

Bizarre bafflegab: Incomprehensible or pretentious verbiage, especially bureaucratic jargon.

Coached to hate.

If utterances simply reiterate the status quo rather than "resist hegemons" the colleges won't protect em.

The left sees heteros as a mixture of hashtags, slutwalks and objectification--so they're all alone.

Violence is the last refuge of the incompetent. Isaac Asimov

Now in universities you can use violence against a speaker's "discursive violence"--they did it first.

Violence is sanctioned by incompetent professors almost like it's self-defense.

Hillary defends character assassination/harassment of the Kavanaugh battle--even for her, unbelievable.

THE COMMUNIST SPIRIT

Construct an entire federal budget to solve a problem that doesn't exist. That's Trudeau, Castro's kid.

No one cares about pronouns/equity except they're worried about what you will take from them, naturally.

It makes me insanely happy to argue with these creeps. I'm way past caring what they think cuz it stinks.

Left will be smearing and destroying anyone who stands in their way. First verbally, then physically.

Stalinist tactic: pretend you don't exist then if that doesn't work, smear you and if needed kill you.

THE YOUTH ARM OF THE DEMOCRATS

They aren't Antifa or Black Lives Matter they're the youth arm of the democratic party and very violent.

They're calling me batshit crazy. They did the same to Palin and Trump for no reason I could see.

Youth are crazy, I mean really sick. They weren't born that way it's their professors/groupthink.

There's no talking to the crazy youth. Liberalism is a mental illness and they have it the worst/uncouth.

They're so ensconced in the liberal mindset they can't see out. They need re-education camps/Trump.

Whatever they say they are it's the opposite. Take the vegans for instance--a cruel bunch called "justice".

To the crazy youth it's all about "equality". So they hurt the dog to be equal to the pig: sadistic thugs.

F--k is now a common word in everyday vernacular since the culture has taken a nosedive morally.

THE COMMUNIST SPIRIT

I refuse to argue or even talk to them cuz they're so disrespectful, without logic or reason, run from them.

I am content now that I have moved to a red state and have land, fence and especially a locked gate.

LET RIGHT DIVIDE FROM FALSE, NOW!

They were wrong, Trump was right, and they're gonna destroy the country for it telling everyone to fight.

Save yourself so much energy. Don't think of them, write or reply to them, argue or debate them.

No Hillary, we don't want to abolish the constitution in favor of your left-wing nut-cake judges.

Save yourself incredible energy by never thinking about em again let alone arguing with em, amen.

Study shows NON-whites don't want political correctness but liberal whites love "anti-racist" censorship.

Thank you dems for bringing republicans together like never before. External conflict = internal solidarity.

You can't argue since it becomes a yelling match, and they bring friends around to really make you mad.

Not only is the left dead wrong they're arrogant in their false crown. It's all gonna hit the fan, clowns.

Social hypnotism is such a dark/strong web that one is moved to accept the narrative. Break out--I did.

They're getting crazier and crazier and this means potentially very violent--you must escape him or her.

I will never leave home unescorted. That's AFTER moving to a red state with a fence and a locked gate.

THE COMMUNIST SPIRIT

Sure Donald is our friend but can he defend us in the end? No cuz it's still Obama's bureaucrats, searchin'

My best advice is to escape the BLUE STATES. They're destined for hell and crashing fast/bad fate.

The most debauched, disordered and awful things and liberals say "things have always been that way".

Even TV ads show everyone filled with tattoos. Think of the fifties--can you imagine the reaction?

First one took right over--a communist spirit. The second one was sweet but mean, little difference.

DIG IN, A CIVIL WAR'S COMING

Gear up/dig in, the Civil War's starting.

A liberal wants to kill em in the womb or later if they make it, cut their genitals off as a transgender kid.

The Jew-hater and Trump-hater is now the poster boy for leftist media propaganda and smear.

What is biggest reason for Trump-hate? Because he said to go to the bathroom that your genitalia dictates.

I just post liberal fake news to inoculate. This is the kinda crap they are saying so face it and transcend it.

Democrats have become the non-white party. But many POCs are leaving since they see the treachery.

Mainstream Fake News Media: "We may have a point of view but not a bias". Hah, what is this.

WHY DO THEY LIE: Cuz those on fake news are paid ridiculous salaries.

If the democrats win, invasion will be endless until America is gone forever. Vote red or be dead.

THE COMMUNIST SPIRIT

One man's death is a tragedy but a million is just a statistic. Stalin

White people must have their own homeland or it's the end.

Communist countries see American gayness as a plot to bring them down but globalists push it son.

Victory: Long jail sentence for worldwide nationalist populist overturned, time for great cheer!

Tommy Robinson is now a right-wing martyr and the left is really pist about losing that place sir.

Martyr freed/revolution has begun!

ANTI-GLOBALISM IS BURGEONING

We're joining with other countries against globalist dehumanizing dynamics and tendencies.

The new trend in Latin America is an abrupt turn to the right and it's nationalism/God almighty.

Why isn't Maxine Waters, Jesse Jackson or the NACP talking about the black genocide in L.A.?

The race hustlers are allowing the obvious black genocide in L.A. to happen for the votes alone.

We're no more a country standing for your demented words of violence and death. Be cautious! Trump

A group can suffer setbacks but as long as it has it's territorial space it can recover.

Champagne socialists push diversity to please the youth while not having to live with the poop.

The effects of multiculturalism are ethnic and cultural displacement.

THE COMMUNIST SPIRIT

Throwing acid in one's face with goal of disfigurement is a foreign and barbaric practice.

Merkel madness is about to topple and I'm so glad she's been murderously awful for her people.

How does evil Soros get his political gain? My overseeing Europe's "managed decline".

Throwing Tommy Robinson into prison population is like throwing a baby to the shark's ocean.

The indigent masses want what you have and that's the BIG DRAW of these socialist candidates.

SOCIALISM APPEALS TO THE DUMB

Socialism appeals to the dumb/low IQ pops who can't learn from history and want your yachts.

Trump is pulling the biggest sting in history.

Democrats have always been socialist--gimme free stuff--they're just now making their move.

If whites don't have babies they'll soon be a minority as their country becomes a ghetto surely.

Europe's decline is rapid and terminal.

Far from being grateful migrants despise Germans.

We're to gladly self-destruct with our first interests global despite what we have to swallow? Hell no.

Political correctness blocked discussion of similarities or differences between groups of people.

Horrible agenda 21 Plan: All the earth's billions of inhabitants will inhabit only 41 megacities.

THE COMMUNIST SPIRIT

Stop blaming or resenting interlopers and put the focus back on you for allowing open borders.

The anti-Brexit anti-Trump liberals gave us the determination to succeed and we finally are now.

WHITE GENOCIDE: BRED OUT OF EXISTENCE

Being bred out of existence is white genocide.

The biggest thing to em is unequal outcomes: If it's not equal we did something to block em.

Every society: Renaissance (blooming phase) then corruption, decadence, weirdness, pyramids.

You know you live in a great country when people who detest it refuse to leave.
Candace Owens

They are communists: they wanna take everything from you and give it to others or themselves.

This is simply horrible. They're killing pets, they're raping everything. God help us soon I pray!

Their arguments have become increasingly sophomoric and opaque as whites are blamed/hated.

The bigger our wall against reality/the less consequences to treachery the less we keep out enemies.

Pope washes feet of a wishy washy internationalist view of Islam.

Just pull the plug they'll self-deport

Works like a top: accused of racism, we pay up.

Tyranny comes in a happy face.

Remain independent of the vicissitudes of demographic change with a fence and locked gate.

THE COMMUNIST SPIRIT

Send them back or they'll keep coming.

Only house/fence/locked gate remains impervious to the vicissitudes of demographic change.

ISOLATE TO AVOID DEMOGRAPHIC DESSTRUCTION

Political Islam is parallel societies and radical tendencies.

Elites want post-industrial austerity with world poverty and a tiny elite tax exempt/diplomatic immunity.

People are waking up all over the world, elections throwing globalists and IMF World Bank Out.

Patriots in the UK don't wanna be ruled by Transylvanian aristocracy or wicca like Theresa Mae.

How is the white man bad if his religion is mocked but he doesn't kill anyone/just sad? END

The only people you're allowed to hate are white.

Whereas it used to be natural to defend borders of a nation now that's nativist, xenophobic, bigoted.

What they used to do with swords they now do with immigrant conquerors.

We lost our defenses when told "they're all good" and to be welcoming to the depraved dunces.

What scares me is Sharia Law and their hatred of dogs.

The effects of multiculturalism are ethnic and cultural displacement.

Freaks me out man. The way they treat animals, that's the barometer of a good/humane culture.

We're going into a very dark time. Thank God I'll be gone but we're seeing the Beginning of the End.

THE COMMUNIST SPIRIT

Give white man a pile of bricks/he'll build a city, give black man a city/he'll build a pile of bricks.

"Race is not a biological construct but a social one" Liberal scientist, insane and dumb.

Liberal myth we hate: We are all the same so should just relax and enjoy giving our country away.

America not Babylon but Nineveh.

LIBERALS LOVE INVADERS AS VOTERS

Despite the obviousness of failed policies the left is compelled to try em again: insanity.

You evil Hungarians dare to want to preserve your own culture. EU stance

Salvini to connect all nationalist parties in Europe to seal the deal--the new direction rid of Merkel.

Well done Matteo Salvini my friend I'd love to buy you a drink sometime or even champagne.

I have felt like the underdog helpless as the foreign invasion goes on without cessation.

They played to the soundbite: "abolish ice"

Who knew that helping the poor could make you so rich.

There's no way for government to make us better, all it can do is make us worse. Derek Hunter

A rising tide raises all boats but a sinking tide sinks em all too just look at Venezuela you fools.

You can have open borders or welfare state but not both cuz they come for free stuff/it's destroyed.

THE COMMUNIST SPIRIT

"Detained children" ginned up by globalists for open borders, cheap labor and democrat voters.

Whole gist: If you don't wanna be separated from your family don't cross the border illegally.

We've gotta have borders and there's consequences if you cross illegally/become a criminal now.

If you don't know your history you get to repeat it until you learn it or you die.

They're displacing Europeans with docile, dependent welfare slaves who won't challenge authority.

DOCILE DEPENDENT WELFARE SLAVES

They don't want integration, it's all about bringing people in who don't want small gov/liberty at all.

Only 3% get jobs, they were brought in as dependent slobs with the goal of socialist control.

Paradise is small government and liberty but these aliens wanna be paid for by you and me.

We used to happily walk to concerts but now worry about knives in a totally different mindset.

There's big money/LOOT in all aspects of climate change and that has corrupted science.

Exporting billions to countries who don't play fair then buy up America. Trump says: no more!

Merkel is a total failure and everyone knows it: "We're sick of you witch, good riddance!"

Don't you wanna control your own destiny? Why prefer some unelected bureaucrat's tyranny?

THE COMMUNIST SPIRIT

If they don't know about private property it's scary cuz they'll take your stuff if given the upper hand.

We all want the EU gone but if their policing of the internet is achieved, we lose and they've won.

In the tyrannical EU today, democracy and opinion is only permitted when you vote the right way.

Those who care more for members of other countries than their own don't love anyone.

SOCIALIST COMMUNIST GLOBALIST

You have no idea how evil the socialist communist Obama is. He demeaned America/all of us.

Liberals want no borders/for America to be crowded with foreign people and they're not evil?

It's gotta be a full-on patriot not some RINO playing the same games as Clinton. Dig deep, amen.

If you're not protecting borders you're also not protecting the inside of the nation, it's values.

Democrats manufactured border hysteria for votes.

Islam the sexist religion of the world, with women 1/2 a man but liberals love it (even the girls).

Race hustlers are cowards on a foundation of lies, Satan's sand. Confront with truth/they run.

Race hustlers speak so fast/smooth you don't know they're lying but they are, making millions.

According to rules you don't go on dole unless here legally for five years yet leeches everywhere.

THE COMMUNIST SPIRIT

In Italy the left has imploded totally and thus marks the direction of other European countries.

The more the left insults us the more the right rewards us. Matteo Salvini

"World Citizen" is the notion pushed by neoMarxists and the UN.: it's all about open borders man.

Nations and cultures no longer matter in a matrix of World Citizenship but we still gotta pay for it.

Go to any elementary school--they see themselves as world citizens not Americans my friends.

Entering a new world of the right--nationalism, populism, traditionalism--and what light!

RUSSIAN YOUTH THE MOST PATRIOTIC

Russian youth are the most pro-Putin, patriotic, nationalistic and religious of any generation, gosh.

Boring, hideous and cruel: becoming a standardized multicultural liberal globalist enterprise.

Sleeper cell traitor Obama, enemy of America

Liberals demand aliens' court hearing but our dear leader says NO--send em back now not later.

The RINO republicans are as bad as democrats, supporting their donors for the open borders.

They want borders in their lives yet not in yours but hypocrisy no more cuz we're in Trump's world.

Enormous amount of black on white violence all across the country and all unreported by the press.

Critical Racism taught in the schools: racism is everywhere and permanent they say to new fools.

THE COMMUNIST SPIRIT

The corporate media hypes racial division 24/7 and the culprit's always the white men.

Liberal news is eliminating comment sections cuz it's all conservative complaints against em.

Fired for telling the **TRUTH** about black-on-white racial violence.

"Around blacks never relax". Employee fired for these words: facts.

Foreign nationals flooding the border are called unaccompanied children as a deceiver.

It's a corporate funded Maoist uprising.

Black on Asian violence is so bad it's called Frisco's "dirty little secret" about poor storeowners.

BUT WHITES DO IT TOO: NOT TRUE

"But whites are doing this too" NOT TRUE.

Lies we bought: Obama introduced concept that all disparity in outcome was white people's fault.

Critical Race Theory: Blacks are relentless victims of relentless white racism--one reality.

Critical race theory (whites are demons) is taught to children let alone colleges where it's Religion.

The greatest lie of this generation is black people are relentless victims of whites the culprits.

Subconscious Racism: We are guilty for something we're not even aware of--that's the plan.

Whites are like evil tigers who are just gonna maul blacks everywhere: that's the myth declared.

THE COMMUNIST SPIRIT

What is a racist? A conservative winning an argument with a liberal. Peter Brimelow

Democrats were the KKK and against equality.

Affirmative Action quotas enormous: the unfairness is damaging while the basis is erroneous.

UK universities tinker with white scores, severely reduce Asian and pump up black, no kiddin'

Affirmative Action theory: you're so bad we've gotta force people to hire you/put you first too.

A black gets into Princeton/must choose: physics/math or Afro resentment in Black schools.

Stop using a hyphen and be an American.

NEVER A MENTION OF WHITE RACISM

White racism unmentioned by never-Trumpers.

Children of the Lie want to bring in non-whites who are socialists from s--thole countries.

The immigrants coming in are brainwashed to hate white people seduced by free stuff/meals.

Children of the Lie seek to reduce white culture by migrants used to tyranny/socialist lures.

They want a black takeover of America and this idea makes us shudder cuz we'll be done, over.

Just look at the violence, lack of respect, nastiness and ghetto dirtiness of the black cities.

Europe is gone, it's over, a ghetto. Don't let it happen to America the greatest country known.

THE COMMUNIST SPIRIT

In Europe whites don't have freedom to disagree with the POCs (people of color). Amazing?

"F--k borders, F--K walls" as left is desperate to start civil war around ICE headquarters.

Merkel is finished, it's just a matter of when. She's ruined Germany so can now enjoy retirement.

The more they go down the Bernie Sanders socialist path the more they'll lose elections/relevance.

The youth want full on socialism but no thank you I want to keep my money not give it to bums.

SOCIALISM IS ALWAYS AUTHORITARIAN

Socialism is inherently authoritarian since you confiscate from me then redistribute for free.

Redistribute until wealthy are bled dry and the impoverished majority becomes a dead country.

Socialism has killed 100 million people in the last century. How can the left want this misery?

Harsh punishments like amputation vs. mercy, forgiveness and salvation then God forgets it son.

What kind of merciful God would chop off something so beautiful as a hand for stealing an egg?

The left are sick freaks--we know that--but violently want open borders to totally wreck us.

Psychologists have become democrat confessors instilling the filthy globalist liberal agenda.

They're at war with prosperity/capitalism, foolish tools of the globalist agenda to take us down.

THE COMMUNIST SPIRIT

Their viewpoint is media-induced and group-controlled--they won't give it up till sick and old.

Beating people over the head with clubs and if you fight back you're a racist.

Collapse third world, put socialist/communists in charge, remove western borders = fascist world.

When college professors light the fuse the most violent revolutions come through students.

When they say "silence is violence" they also tell us what not to be silent about--important to see this.

AGEISM IS WORSE THAN RACISM

In an ageist society they judge you by age. It's worse than racism since you're at the top of your game.

The entire time I knew you I was made conscious of my age. That's ageism man, inapropos for a sage.

No matter your big plans, God still puts one up just as He puts another down. Success is from Him man.

The burden the Lord takes from us is the catastrophe of bad memories. Pray for this: please change history.

Don't abandon TV. I love the History/war documentaries, old classic movies and Tucker/Laura/Hannity.

The burden of bad memories is cast on the Lord. My biggest care tho' not there and couldn't go forward.

Paul took it as his MAIN goal: to forget ALL that lay behind and concentrate on what lies ahead, that's all.

It was California or Vegas, you swam in muddy waters in hypnosis, you were in a fog like all addicts.

THE COMMUNIST SPIRIT

All those dry years I never knew I had it in me but now I'm a constant spring, just be ever-ready.

It's the Christian paradigm: the one called a FOOL turns out being the biggest success of this world.

It's uncanny how the serial bully in a family can literally pick off lives until they're all gone without a memory.

First she killed her husband thru calumny, isolation and false accusation. Then mother/sister, all gone.

You had me in a trance but now the spell is gone. I'm so grateful for this, I prayed for it for so long.

I guess I'm super-suggestible being a triple Pisces but I'm not into astrology as God's above it all, see?

HIX POLITIX IS TRAGIC

White subservience: You are making obvious fools of yourselves. Stand up, you didn't hold slaves.

Forced to share and other signs of the communist spirit made us sick from kindergarten on/bewitched.

Hypocrisy, sick: You can go out and violently protest but you can't get together since it's a covid risk.

Hitler's incredible self-belief was ignited by his gift for public speaking. 60 million dead, imagine.

It's not so much liberal vs. conservative but two entirely separate and parallel news universes.

It's really about "pansexuality": sex with anything, the same sex, animal, a hole in the wall.

The Antifa and BLM Syndicate are funded by the same people intent on destroying America.

THE COMMUNIST SPIRIT

BLM is actually Antifa inciting black rage in a created crisis then focusing the violence in prescribed ways.

Big major corporations better right fat checks or be called insensitive at best, racist at worst.

Aren't we sick of having to tip toe around Marxists masquerading as humanitarians?

Now they're telling us that worrying about home invasions is racist? It's all from our white privilege.

They could come and take you outa your homes if they ever got power. Real power, head honcho.

Defunding the police brings on the protection racket: gangs with guns running around, tragic.

GUESS I'M A WRITER

It's what I do: all day and night long. I didn't choose it I just fell into my groove based on ancestral wisdom.

The writing goes on and on all day long with half hour breaks when God says "go sit in the sun".

I'm a writer, I write all day long. Writers may not want to be seen or interviewed if it's not where they belong.

It's all about the COPY--the words lasting beyond the passing of the writer. So interviews, why ever?

Your groove is as natural as a bird singing to you. Find it to have prosperity, fine homes and lovely views.

To think/write clearly I gotta let you go. What you think I don't wanna know cuz destiny is here not below.

A singer sings, a painter paints, a writer writes and at a certain point it's constant all day and night.

THE COMMUNIST SPIRIT

To write like that you must have a firm foundation—the hero's path of trials/tribulations then jubilation.

I love to hear what a true singer sings or see what a true painter paints cuz natural talents are divine I think.

Too bad they can't just learn it from words like it used to be. Now they have to see the person sorry to say.

It should just be your work—books, concerts, paintings—not your mug in a video talking about insanity.

You wanna be seen, I don't. I'm not into that cuz I know time changes all things—I want ETERNITY.

CONTENT CREATORS

Acting like you know everything when you seem to know nothing. Taking credit like it's you all along.

Making a big deal out of trifles, boring us with the details. Get a life: pick your high times to make videos.

You can't make a good video just cuz you want to, at a certain time too. You WAIT to work, cued.

I couldn't care less about the stuff you talk about so it's at this point I'll bow out. The internet is infinite, ciao.

People don't understand you create thru subtraction, not addition. They keep adding on to its ruination.

By now you can see the routine. It's more or less constant while taking breaks looking at the scenery.

FINAL FRUITARIANISM

Cats are precious/affectionate. The more they're loved the more unique personalities come out.

THE COMMUNIST SPIRIT

The depression was a partial fast not a full one and people regained their perfect health hon'

They ate whatever they found in the depression. It wasn't a complete fast but healed nevertheless.

So if you break your fast by eating again don't be let down, you're equally healed by a partial one.

One good thing about fruitarianism is you need little--it's frugal. Not gluttony of fruit, that's a NO.

Make up dense calories with dates and bananas if you need more. Spuds/noodles didn't work.

ROLLING 48 [EAT EVERY OTHER DAY]

The Rolling 48 or Eat Every Other Day Diet gets easier with time and the fast day becomes sublime.

We got our patio awning up so I'll be writing out in the sun with beautiful mountain views as a backdrop.

Poetry, dog tennis, music, housekeeping, sitting out with the view. It's a full life and all I ever do.

It's all splendid were it not ruined daily with bad memories but I know the Lord doesn't want it that way.

Viewed thru the prism of the past I'm always degraded in image and it's embarrassing too I guess.

In the female sex triggers bonding hormones. That makes her the vulnerable one to put the brakes on.

When you repent of your sins God gives you total knowledge: you're now an endless spout.

It may take a woman half her life just to get her mother out of her. In this case the older is better.

Lord, take bad memories off our back. They trigger adrenalin/keep us drained so take em, *thanks*.